DUNDURN CASTLE

Sir Allan MacNab and his Hamilton Home

EDWARD SMITH

James Lorimer & Company Ltd., Publishers
Toronto

Text Copyright © 2007 Edward Smith
Visuals Copyright © 2007 James Lorimer & Company Ltd.

All rights reserved. No part of this book may be reproduced or transmitted in any form or by any means, electronic or mechanical, including photocopying, or by any information storage or retrieval system, without permission in writing from the publisher.

James Lorimer & Company Ltd. acknowledges the support of the Ontario Arts Council. We acknowledge the support of the Government of Canada through the Book Publishing Industry Development Program (BPIDP) for our publishing activities. We acknowledge the support of the Canada Council for the Arts for our publishing program. We acknowledge the support of the Government of Ontario through the Ontario Media Development Corporation's Ontario Book Initiative.

James Lorimer & Company Ltd., Publishers
317 Adelaide Street West, Suite #1002
Toronto, ON
M5V 1P9
www.lorimer.ca

Printed and bound in Canada

Library and Archives Canada Cataloguing in Publication

Smith, Edward Arthur Warwick, 1951-
  Dundurn Castle : Sir Allan MacNab and his Hamilton home / Edward Smith.

Includes bibliographical references.
ISBN 978-1-55028-988-6

  1. MacNab, Allan Napier, Sir, 1798–1862.
2. Dundurn Castle (Hamilton, Ont.) — History.
3. MacNab, Allan Napier, Sir, 1798–1862 — Homes and haunts — Ontario — Hamilton.
4. Statesmen — Canada — Biography.
5. Ontario. Legislative Assembly — Biography.
6. Businessmen — Ontario — Hamilton — Biography. 7. Hamilton (Ont.) — Biography. I. Title.

FC3098.8.D85S6 2007   971.3'5202092
C2007-904964-8

Contents

Floor Plans   4

Part I: Sir Allan MacNab's Castle: A Walking Tour   5

Part II: The Life of Sir Allan MacNab
    Introduction   47
    Early Life and Character   49
    A Canadian Dundurn   55
    Change in the Air   67
    "All My Politics Are Railroads"   75
    MacNab the Moderate   85

Epilogue   91
Acknowledgements   93
Sources   94

Floor Plans

Upper Floor

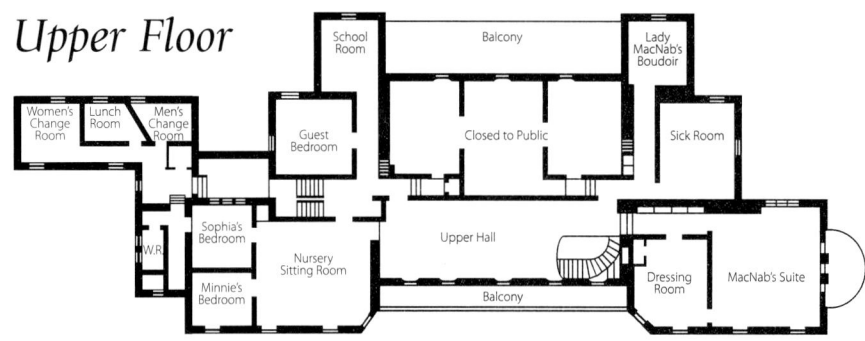

Main Floor

Basement

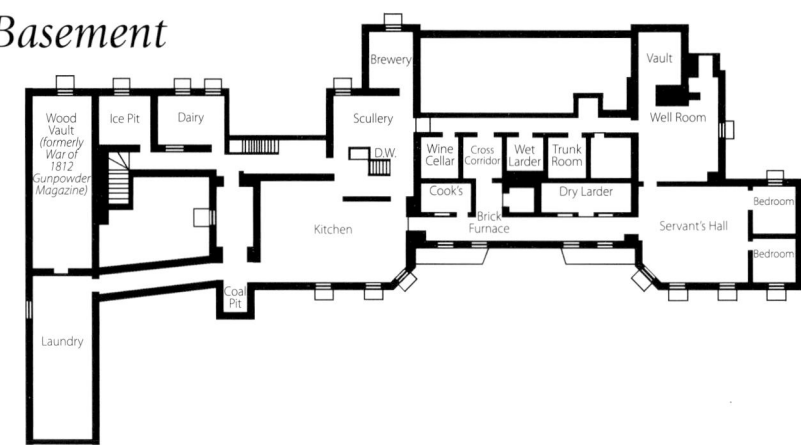

Part I
Sir Allan MacNab's Castle

Dundurn Castle sits high overlooking Burlington Bay at the very western end of Lake Ontario. The house is usually seen as one enters or leaves Hamilton by the old York Road, though when it was built its architect, Robert Wetherell, meant this Italianate fantasy in white to be viewed from the bay. Wetherell was an English architect who had settled in Hamilton in the early 1830s. Wetherell and Sir Allan Napier MacNab, the house's owner, a man who would become Hamilton's most famous historic citizen, wanted to make their mark on colonial society by choosing a design for the home that was not merely in fashion, but in advance of it in Canada. MacNab was a man with one foot in the eighteenth century and the other in the nineteenth — an entrepreneur who wanted a house that would demonstrate not just his wealth, but his family history.

Front entrance to Dundurn Castle

Dundurn Castle

MacNab was a descendant of impoverished Highland chiefs. The ancestral Dundurn was on Loch Earn in Perthshire, Scotland, a rude hill fort, used for bloody and vicious raids on rival clans such as the MacNeishes, but it was a seat with a claim to nobility. In Hamilton, Dundurn would be a home fit for a New-World laird and his lady — his second wife, Mary — his children, and a shifting assortment of relatives.

Houses have long been a way for the wealthy to present their image of themselves to the world. In eighteenth-century England, the labouring classes might rent small cottages or live as tenants in rural villages, and the middling people might live in row townhouses in the new cities, but the aristocracy constructed, decorated, and landscaped so-called "great houses" throughout the countryside, competing with each other to reflect their own greatness. MacNab's great house was a statement of an age that was already passing; it asserted his rank in a world where noble birth and blue blood still commanded a respect born of centuries of deference. Allan MacNab would

Inset: Chief of the clan MacNab
Above: Architect Robert Wetherell's drawing of Dundurn, 1841

enter the Victorian age of steam and industry with entrepreneurial verve, but his house told of a different side of his personality: he was a man who felt at home in a more deferential age, that of the Regency, which spoke of "orders" of society; of a society divided into ordered ranks of deference based on birth. All his dealings — political, financial, entrepreneurial — were designed to move the New World MacNabs up in this older concept of society. Dundurn was the centre and heart of this need.

Today Dundurn's setting is a park, but in the beginning its grounds were a working farm, designed to support its family. The home was surrounded by orchards and lawns, and contained a working dairy, kitchens, and a brewery. It was beautiful to behold, both inside and out, but fully practical too. In its rooms and designs, Dundurn reveals Canada in the early nineteenth century — its people, its social relationships, and most importantly, this country's dreams. Like the newest great houses in Britain, Dundurn was designed to be looked upon, and to look outward. It had ground-floor windows that looked out on the picturesque grounds and could be swung open and stepped through out onto the lawns. Country gentlemen had only recently acquired the habit of appreciating nature. Though Allan MacNab dealt in railroads, steamships, politics, and trade, the purpose of all these activities was to provide for his life as a country gentleman.

It is a relatively narrow house, constructed on the foundations of an earlier house built for one of Hamilton's first residents, Richard Beasley. Beasley, a fur trader, had built a Loyalist colonial brick house — itself large for the times — with outbuildings, an orchard, and docks below on the bay. MacNab's conviction that the future was firmest when built on the past would not allow him to obliterate the first house on the site. So, because the Beasley house was narrow, Dundurn is narrow too, a characteristic that affects the layout of the large ground-floor ceremonial rooms but is not easily noticeable from outside.

With Wetherell's blueprints and his own aspirations guiding him, MacNab began construction in 1833, and the building was substantially complete by 1835. MacNab had been in Hamilton only nine years at this point. He had lost one wife and their son, married again, and had two more daughters, half-sisters for the surviving older daughter from his first marriage. He was a prosperous, engaging, and successful lawyer and entrepreneur. His new house reflected all this.

The bricks were moulded and fired on the site, a common practice then, usually carried out by ordinary labourers, and the wood and stone were purchased. A local master builder, Luther Smith, was in charge of the construction. He hired masons, carpenters, latherers, and plasterers. In typical MacNab fashion, these workmen were paid, at least partially, with land. As time would attest, they built well.

The earliest architecture in the colony was a copy of American neoclassical forms familiar in the old Thirteen Colonies, now the United States. Whether small log houses in the bush or newer stone residences in villages and towns, they had similar features. A centrally placed doorway opened to a centre hallway. Rooms branched out on either side, and the windows were placed in regular order to each side. This was the facade of order and reason so loved in the rational, enlightened eighteenth century. Richard Beasley's house on Burlington Heights was a brick vision of this style. But something new was stirring in the early nineteenth century: the Romantic movement. John Nash had designed his first Italianate house, Cronkhill, in Shropshire in 1802. This style had elements of neoclassical regularity, combined with whimsy, and was to remain popular in England to the middle of the nineteenth century, when neo-Gothic architecture became dominant.

Dundurn Castle

Drawing room

Dundurn was, in other words, on the cutting edge of fashion, especially notable in a small, rough town like Hamilton, Upper Canada. Other Italianate houses and buildings were to be erected in British North America prior to Confederation, but none were as remarkable, nor as early, as Dundurn.

The internal design of the house reflects the love of the Classical Revival style then in vogue, best exemplified by the fireplace mantelpieces, which were a later embellishment. During MacNab's lifetime the home underwent renovations, so that it kept pace with the changes in the family's needs and tastes. The house is Canadian, too. The rooms can be closed off as self-contained units, to minimize drafts and keep heat in as much as possible during the cold Canadian winters. There are two staircases: a magnificent black walnut "flying" staircase joining the entrance and upper halls, and a simpler "back" stair, used by children and servants. While the rich in Britain were building houses with servants' wings, Dundurn followed an older model that placed the working part of the house in a basement, though perhaps this choice was more a reflection of a growing Canadian trend in house building, which used basements as work spaces. Today, visitors are impressed with the large public rooms of Dundurn, especially the dining room. But the servants' below-stairs workrooms and living spaces fascinate as well, because here the working Dundurn is on display.

Approaching the Castle

Modern visitors usually see the house first from York Street. From this vantage point, the columned portico at this entrance is the home's most striking feature, but it was not part of Wetherell's original design. It was a later addition, built in 1855 as part of the preparations for the wedding of MacNab's middle daughter, Sophia, to William Coutts Keppel, Viscount Bury. Sir Allan hired the architect Frederick Rastrick to design this feature, which also required the redesign and rebuilding of the doorway to match. As one writer has suggested, the portico announced to the world that the bride was not just the daughter of a successful man, but of a prime minister. With long, French casement windows set on either side of the entrance, and smaller casement windows spaced regularly along the second floor above, the portico thus framed presents an image of a Greek or Roman temple set against a backdrop of a Tuscan villa. A long circular drive allowed passengers to emerge from their carriages virtually at the doorstep, and then enter the house through the main doors under the shelter of the portico. Entrance gates were added to the property in 1855; they had been built for another local luminary, George Rolph, in Dundas, but never used. It was after these features had been added that Dundurn began to be called Dundurn Castle.

Main entrance

The Entrance Hall

MacNab's insistence that Dundurn be built on the base of Richard Beasley's narrow neoclassical brick cottage meant that the larger rooms would be long and narrow. The first space that guests see upon stepping over the threshold of Dundurn Castle is indeed long and narrow, stretching along an east-west axis. The wall facing the door was lined with family portraits, chairs, and a couch. This centre wall separated it from the formal dining room to the north. Guests would have been met at the door by Wellington, the butler. Gentlemen's hats and walking sticks were placed in the stand by the door. An oil cloth protected the floor from muddy or snowy boots and shoes in bad weather. The butler directed the guests to their right, to the drawing room, past the grand staircase that leads to the family rooms on the second floor. The walls were papered and the floor tiled, a formal but rather plain decor compared with that of the other public rooms. The grand hallway was a place for conversation as guests and family mingled at the start of a social evening, or where business partners or political colleagues chatted amiably before getting down to business in other rooms.

Above: Painting of Sir Allan MacNab in the entrance hall
Above right: Grandfather clock in the entrance hall
Opposite page: Staircase in the grand hallway

The Drawing Room

The drawing room is one of the loveliest rooms in the house. Despite its formal decoration, the carpeting, furniture, and especially the long windows, give the room a coziness and comfort that visitors must have appreciated. Overstuffed chairs, with a two-sided sofa as their centrepiece, hugged the walls, which were hung with pictures. Tables were adorned with the bric-a-brac that was becoming common even in early Victorian times.

It was likely warmer than some rooms, as it faced east, away from the prevailing winds, and looked out onto the estate and the front drive. Here the family entertained guests formally, usually before and after dining. The room had a piano, one of several in the house that MacNab's daughters Sophia and Minnie used in their music lessons with Charles Ambrose, who was the organist in the 1840s at Hamilton's Anglican parish, Christ's Church. In the days before radio and television, family and guests created their own entertainment, singing and making music together. In this room in 1855, Sophia was married to William Keppel, Viscount Bury. It was converted to a chapel for the early-morning Catholic ceremony and again for the later, more formal Church of England wedding. That night, it became a ballroom for the celebration.

Below: Drawing room chaise
Opposite page: Luxurious furnishings in the drawing room

MacNab's Office, Library, and Smoking Room

Tucked into the northeast corner of the house are the only rooms that were specifically set aside for Allan MacNab's use. His office and library seem surprisingly small, cramped, and dark for a man who had so many business and political interests. The darkness came from the liberal use of black walnut, also from a renovation in 1847. Opening onto the entrance hall, giving visitors easy access to it, the office would not have been a very private space, though much of Sir Allan's business was conducted in the legislature, or in face-to-face contact with partners in his railways and in the local Gore Bank, which he partially owned. If these quarters seemed confining, Sir Allan could open the windows and step outside into the grounds for a stroll, perhaps to think, or to talk more confidentially with partners. Off to one side was his library — not quite a separate room, but

MacNab's desk

Decanter in McNab's office

14

an area with enough space and shelving to hold a collection of more than 300 books. He had a varied collection, though it is not known whether the books were for show, or actually consulted or enjoyed by MacNab. There were basic law books, books on the aristocracy, books on history, on travel, theology, newspapers, parliamentary journals, and fiction. Notable among them were the complete works of Sir Walter Scott, and several volumes on Scottish history, especially of the Highlands. All were auctioned off after his death.

MacNab's office and library

Just past the office is his smoking room, which although quite small looks out over the north lawn towards the bay, and is equipped for enjoying a cigar and a glass of port or other wine. Tenants and those who owed MacNab money would tap on the window here to get his attention and enter to pay bills, or settle accounts — those who owed the laird did not enter by the grand hallway.

One suspects many of his deals were cemented in these close, but convivial quarters, perhaps in winter when walks in the grounds were not possible. Incongruously to us today, these spaces are sometimes referred to as a boudoir.

During MacNab's first years in Hamilton, before Dundurn, he had law offices in the town. After Dundurn was built, MacNab spent most of his time in land speculation, the promotion of railroads, and politics. His library contained his law books, but he spent little time after the 1830s in practice. Mostly he was out meeting people, and making deals.

Archaeological investigations carried out in the 1990s indicate that MacNab's offices were first located in the western end of the first floor, suggesting that this was the first actively used space in the house while building was still under way. His office and vault for record storage were moved to the east end of the house on the south side when the building was completed. After the 1847 renovations, the offices moved to the northeast location, and the vault moved to the basement.

The Grand Dining Room

The dining room is a long, narrow room, mirroring the entrance hall on the other side of the middle wall. It holds with ease an impressive table and distinctive sideboards inset into alcoves at the ends of the room. In the house as initially built, the alcoves contained serving tables. In the 1847 renovation by the architect Henry Bower Lane, large black walnut sideboards were built and installed. At the west end, two doors flank the alcove — one leading to the butler's room and pantry, the other, back into the entrance hall. By the east alcove, one of the two doors flanking it leads to the entrance hall, the other to a storage room. These too may have dated to the 1847 renovation, but accurate and

Above left: Dining room sideboard
Above right: Silver candelabra in dining room
Opposite page: The grand dining room

specific details of the work are gone. The room was truly grand, with a candle-burning chandelier. Today the chandelier is electric. In the 1847 renovation, MacNab also purchased cylinders to provide gas lighting. No doubt one of the rooms lit was the din-

Above left: Portrait of Queen Victoria in the grand dining room
Above right: Silver centrepiece
Left: Wine cooler

The Grand Dining Room

Paintings of Sir Allan MacNab and Lady MacNab hanging in the dining room attributed to R. Whale

ing room, to illuminate the evening parties.

The table could seat as many as two dozen, including the host and hostess. The host's chair at the head of the table was notable for its gout stool. Sir Allan suffered much from this ailment late in life, and was sometimes almost crippled by it. The view of the grounds to the north and the bay through the room's large French-door windows stole the show; guests who were so unfortunate as to be seated with their backs to the windows were comforted by facing the large fireplace and the portraits of the Queen and her consort, Prince Albert, hanging to the right of it.

The room was not always so formal. When she was thirteen, MacNab's middle daughter, Sophia, noted in her diary for January 22, 1846, "We could not have our lessons in the dining room so we had them in the nursery," indicating that the schoolmaster, Mr. Thompson, sometimes taught her and her younger sister, Minnie, here. Some evenings, Sophia sat sewing in the dining room. She liked to arrange fruit and flowers for the table when her father had business partners and other important people to dinner. In 1860, during his tour of Canada, Albert Edward, the Prince of Wales, and Sir Edmund Walker Head, the governor general, lunched at Dundurn. This was the high point for Dundurn as a great house.

The Butler's Room and the Pantry

Dumb waiter in the pantry to the right

The butler was the chief servant in the house, and the only to live on the main floor. He was also the only male servant to live in the main house. His room is strategically located just off the dining room, at the end opposite Sir Allan's library, and near the pantry. It is small, barely large enough to hold its single bed, a dresser, and a small stove for heat, but it has a superb view out over the grounds. Unlike the family's rooms, or the common rooms, which had either tile or carpeted floors, it had the wide, painted floorboards seen in more ordinary pioneer homes. Yet it was also a comfortable room.

The pantry contained the house's store of china and silver, which fell to the butler to keep safe and prepare for dinners. Wellington, Allan MacNab's long-time butler, was thus always nearby, to be in attendance on formal occasions in the dining room, or to attend MacNab himself on the same floor. The room has a dumb waiter to bring meals prepared in the basement kitchen up for service by the butler. On the occasions when Wellington accompanied Sir Allan on his frequent trips to parliament, little Sophia would sometimes help serve dinner, which she described in her diary as "fun." Outside the pantry is the back staircase, which was used more often than the grand staircase by both servants and family, and sometimes called the children's staircase. Sir Allan's second wife, Mary Stuart, was ill in the 1840s with what was probably tuberculosis. During this period, everyone used the children's staircase as much as possible, as it was farther from the sickroom on the other side of the house on the second floor, to avoid disturbing Lady Mary's rest.

20

Aunt Sophia's Sitting Room

Aunt Sophia was the sister of MacNab's second wife, Lady Mary, and married to MacNab's younger brother, David Archibald MacNab. When David died in 1840, Sophia came to live at Dundurn. Before her arrival, her sitting room probably served as a small dining room. She took charge of the household when her sister became ill. It was traditional for a woman, usually a man's wife, to take charge of the complicated affairs of running a household, be it large or small. Among her responsibilities were seeing that the children were raised properly and that the servants were doing their tasks. The position was not unlike running a small business, except that financial decisions remained with the father of the family. During some periods, when Lady Mary was feeling better, she took back the reins. After Lady Mary's death from her illness in 1846, Aunt Sophia ran the household until Allan MacNab's death in 1862. She was then executrix of his estate.

This is the small suite from which she ran the house. Sophia's two rooms were comfortable and the largest next to those of Sir Allan and his dying wife on the second floor. The placement of Aunt Sophia's suite on the main floor reflected her position. Her sitting room was near both the entrance hall and the pantry. It was used also as an informal family dining room. Her bedroom was rather more private, with a dressing screen and a hip bath. Ladies did not use the ablution room, but had hot water carried to the bath in their rooms. The constant visitors and young family meant that rooms were not so private as we expect

Aunt Sophia's vanity table

today. Sometimes the girls would sit and sew or read in their aunt's sitting room, or sleep in her bedroom when visitors took other rooms.

The Ablutions Room

Dundurn Castle was a home with all the modern conveniences. The ablutions room had water pumped in under pressure to a large bathtub, a luxury we consider ordinary today. A neat, Classical Revival fireplace kept this small room warm. A small boiler heated water for that ultimate luxury, the hot bath. A wash basin of Doulton china (not yet Royal Doulton) complemented the tub. Even more luxurious was the early indoor flush toilet in its own little room, the soon-to-be-common water closet.

Such a room was a rarity in this period, found only in the homes of the very rich in Britain, and it must have been quite a sensation in 1830s Canada.

Tub with hot water heater

Doulton china wash basin

The Upper Hall

The upper hall is reached using the grand, black walnut "flying" staircase, which brings one to the end of the house outside the master bedroom. With the same dimensions as the entrance hall directly beneath it, this hall is carpeted and decorated in a softer tone, giving it a more spacious and less formal feeling. Despite the wallpaper pattern mimicking stone and the Greek-style niche and statue near the top of the staircase, the carpeting and large, bright windows, and the piano where Sophia and Minnie sometimes had their lessons with Mr. Ambrose, lighten and brighten the space enormously. Altogether, the impression is that there was considerably less formality on the family floor.

The upper hall

MacNab's Rooms

Sir Allan MacNab's rooms, a bedroom with a separate, connected dressing room, are the largest private area in the house. It is not certain whether Sir Allan and Lady MacNab had shared the room before her illness, but in any case it was not unusual in aristocratic families for husband and wife to have separate rooms, if not entire suites. MacNab's suite adjoins Lady MacNab's rooms, and has a separate dressing area, another common feature in aristocratic households of

Above: MacNab's dressing room
Opposite page: MacNab's bed

Desk in MacNab's room

the time. By the 1840s, the suite was called "Papa's room" by young Sophia in her diary. The main room contains a desk where Sir Allan could write his correspondence or take care of some business without being too far from Lady MacNab next door. The dressing room provided a fully private space, where Wellington the butler would assist Sir Allan in dressing and undressing, another common aristocratic practice.

The furniture is heavy and solid-looking, conveying a sense of permanence. The towels on the stand, the porcelain tub for foot soaks, and another gout stool by his easy chair provided MacNab with some relief from the gout, in the relative privacy of his own room, though his daughters were often there with him, reading or

Towel rack in MacNab's room

sewing to keep him company. Little Sophia on occasion slept there also, in the unusual three-poster bed, when her room was taken by visitors, and her father was not home. During the Victorian era, privacy became accepted as normal, but MacNab's house displayed a comfortable familiarity among the residents that tells of an earlier, more public era, in personal relationships. During Lady Mary's illness and Sir Allan's frequent attacks of gout, the children would take turns with their Aunt Sophia sitting with one or the other of their parents and helping them. Sophia sometimes slept in the large bed with Papa, occasionally on short notice, "Nanny came in & asked me if I would not sleep in papa's room that night ... Papa slept very badly."

Lady MacNab's Rooms

This room is where Lady MacNab spent the last period of her life, tended by her family and with frequent calls from both physicians and Catholic clergy. She seldom left her bed in her last months, only sometimes moving to sit in the large chair in the room, or on a sofa. Her bed was equipped with an ingenious table, similar to those used in hospitals today, but considerably more attractive in its polished wood, allowing her to eat or to write without leaving bed.

In better times, she used her small boudoir, which was connected to this room, and positioned exactly above Sir Allan's own private smoking and drinking room. It had a small table for tea or needlework, and a bright north window. When home, Sir Allan was never far away, the master bedroom being next door. It is possible these two rooms were always her own suite, next to Sir Allan's. The children were often here with their mother, or in MacNab's rooms close by, when not taking lessons or music training.

Medical science could hardly be called that in this period. Treatment for most ailments involved "bleeding," or bloodletting, as doctors believed that health was a matter of a proper balance of bodily fluids and that ill health was related to an excess of blood. Small surgery was performed by local doctors — without anaesthesia, though often with a sedative of some sort. Anne Jane, Sir Allan's daughter by his first marriage to Elizabeth Brooke, had a lump removed from behind her ear. "It gave her a great deal of pain, but she bore it well," Sophia wrote in her diary.

The sick room does not look like a hospital room to our eyes, but merely a comfortable room where Lady MacNab could get as much rest as possible, and where a physician could see her in privacy. There was no hospital in Hamilton until 1848, and that was more a place to warehouse the indigent poor than to heal the sick, certainly not the aristocratic sick. Hospitals were dangerous places for years to come, as knowledge of the causes of disease, and even an understanding of germs and infection, was still in the future. For example, hand washing by physicians and surgeons was a disputed novelty in the 1840s.

Lady MacNab was better off in her own room in her own house than anyplace else in the world in those days. Tuberculosis was identified around this time, but there were no effective treatments until well into the twentieth century, and no preventive measures either. Physicians relied on a long list of concoctions, usually made from various roots and herbs, to be either drunk or applied as poultices. The attending physician would bring these treatments in his bag, or order them from a pharmacy in town. For Lady MacNab, the attending physician was usually Dr. James Hamilton, the husband of one of her nieces, or Dr. John King of Toronto, who was married to a cousin. On January 22, 1846, thirteen-year-old Sophia wrote in her diary: "After our lessons were over Aunt Sophia went to town to

Opposite page: The sick room

Chair in the sick room

have the mixture dispensed which Dr. Hamilton had left." Most patient care was comfort rather than cure — soothing cloths for the forehead, light, tasty food to tempt an invalid's appetite, and the loving company of one's family, not perhaps a bad prescription even today.

It is likely that it was here, or in the boudoir, that "dear Mamma," her sister Aunt Sophia, and her two daughters, Sophia and Minnie, would receive communion from the local Catholic priest who came to the house for this purpose during Lady Mary's illness. On at least one occasion, the Catholic bishop Michael Power travelled from Toronto to see her. In better times, Lady MacNab, her two daughters, and her sister attended St. Mary's Catholic Church in the town, while Sir Allan and his elder daughter, Anne Jane, went to Christ's Church Anglican.

The School Room

Education was a haphazard affair in early Canada. There was very little public financial support for schools, and in any case, the children of high-ranking citizens or the well-to-do often received their elementary education at home, from private tutors hired by their parents. There were some elite private schools for older students — boys only — called grammar schools, which were roughly the same as today's high schools or private schools on the English model. John Strachan, the first Anglican bishop of Toronto, began his career in Canada running such schools in Kingston, Cornwall, and finally York. He had pushed for and saw passed laws in 1807 and 1816 that provided some funding for schools. Meanwhile, girls from aristocratic families, such as Minnie and Sophia, were taught at home to read and write and introduced to other languages and music.

The school room is equipped with another piano, and a flute — the two instruments girls were expected to learn, though the piano was the more important. They were not expected to have a career, other than marriage and the household management that entailed. Their education was to prepare them to be good wives to well-connected, prosperous husbands. Sir Allan himself had attended the school run by John Strachan in York. Sir Allan hired a teacher from Strachan's school, Mr. Thompson, to teach Sophia and Minnie at home in the school room. Girls, especially, were expected to be musical, so Mr. Ambrose from Hamilton's only Anglican parish, Christ's Church, came to give piano

School room

lessons. Christ's Church was supported by Sir Allan and designed by Robert Wetherell, the architect who designed Dundurn. Wetherell's design for the church was a neat, white, frame building with a spire; it was later replaced by the stone structure that still exists on James Street North in Hamilton.

The Children's Rooms

This set of rooms, a large nursery flanked by two small bedrooms, was the main living area for the children — comfortably close by but separate from their parents' rooms on the family floor. Dundurn was a living house, and rooms changed their function as needed. The nursery was no longer needed as such by mid century, and was used more as a sitting room, where the girls could practise lessons, or do needlework. The two small bedrooms for Sophia and Minnie were sometimes needed for guests, in which case Sophia and Minnie bunked either with their

Bed in children's room

The Children's Rooms

father or in Aunt Sophia's suite on the main floor. One such visitor was Lady Mary's doctor, James Hamilton, who sometimes stayed the night when travelling conditions were poor.

The nursery is called that, but early in 1846 Sophia notes in her diary, "We decided to give papa the nursery and let Mamma have her own room once more," suggesting Lady MacNab had been sleeping in the second-floor nursery, or perhaps that Sir Allan and Lady MacNab had been sharing the suite of rooms we now call MacNab's rooms, but her deteriorating health meant that "Papa" moved out and into the nursery for a time. It is from confusing entries such as these, which read like a game of musical rooms, that curators have tried to discover the purposes of these rooms.

Top: The nursery
Above: Chamber pot in the children's room

The Kitchen, Scullery, and Brewery

Down the back stairs at the west end of the house are the rooms where the work of Dundurn was carried out. Only some servants would appear upstairs, as a strict upstairs-downstairs physical separation reinforced the social hierarchy. Orders to the lowest level of servants would be transmitted through the butler or the cook, whose jobs included day-to-day supervision. The

Open hearth in kitchen

The Kitchen, Scullery, and Brewery

The scullery

lady of the house, whether that was Lady MacNab or Aunt Sophia, only spoke to lower servants directly when serious discipline was called for. The main staircase does not serve the basement at all — it can be reached only by the back stairs. To the west are the main working rooms, principally the kitchen, the scullery, where dishes, glasses, cutlery, and pots and pans are cleaned, and the brewery where the ordinary drink of the house was produced. In the early years, besides the cook and the butler, there were several housemaids and a children's nurse. It is likely there was a core of permanent servants and that others were hired and fired as MacNab's fortunes followed their roller-coaster course.

Servants were known only by their first names — the butler, Wellington, and the cook, Old Anne, are mentioned in young Sophia's diary. A row of bells connected the kitchen to the main family rooms of the house on both upper floors. Servants were usually illiterate, so the bells were not labelled, but each was of a slightly different size, and thus tone. The servants would have to memorize which tone went with which room, so they could respond when called by bell. In the main rooms, the bells were not pulled (as in old movies) but cranked with a small handle and wheel assembly.

The kitchen, like the ablutions room upstairs, was thoroughly advanced technologically. It con-

Bells in kitchen that chimed for each room

tains both an older, open-hearth fireplace for roasting (using various spits and roasters, some quite ingenious), and a modern iron stove, for baking and other cooking, placed at opposite ends of the long room. The example now in the house dates from after MacNab's time, but gives a good idea of the type, as stoves were a main product of Hamilton, beginning in the mid-nineteenth century. The middle of the room contains a working table, with counter space and storage off to each side — but with room for several servants to move about, preparing, cooking, and placing items into the dumb waiter to send up to Wellington waiting above outside the dining room, or to Aunt Sophia's room, when it was used for informal meals. Both smaller family meals and large formal, multiple-course dinners could be prepared here.

The scullery is located beside the kitchen to the north — it was one of the busiest parts of the servants' domain. The youngest female servant was in charge of washing the less valuable crockery and cooking dishes here. She was usually only twelve or thirteen years old, and her employment in such a household would give her a warm place to live and plenty of food to eat, as well as a modest income.

The small brewery was just beyond the scullery and directly underneath the butler's bedroom. The distinctive odour of malt and hops must have seeped up into Wellington's room on a regular basis. Ale-brewing was the norm, as lagers require cold fermentation, and the British habit was for ale, not lager. Beer in general was the usual drink in an age where water could not be trusted, as the brewing process involved boiling. Indeed, a ration of beer was part of the pay for the young scullery maid. It is difficult to say how strong this beer was — an old practice was to reuse the malt for several brewings, each subsequent batch being weaker. Perhaps children were given the weakest brews, while adults drank the first and strongest, which could be as much as 10 percent alcohol. But the house was cold, and the work for the servants hard, and likely burned off the effects of alcohol. The brewing process killed bacteria, making beer a safe and pleasant drink. Lady MacNab regularly had a glass of beer with oysters for her lunch. The room is quite small, with its own water pump, and just enough space for the brewing vessels and a few barrels. It is not known which servant did the brewing, but the old tradition was for women to brew beer.

The Dairy and the Ice Pit

Of all the castle's rooms, these show best the self-sufficiency of Dundurn. The dairy, where milk and cheese from estate cows were prepared, has white counters and soft light from a window, giving the impression of calm and cleanliness that one expects in such a room. Evidence of the care taken to keep insects and dust out of dairy products is found in the domed screen that was placed over cheeses and butter. A lead-lined container kept these cold — as did the placement of the dairy next to the ice pit.

The ice pit seems bottomless — a stone-lined chamber where one can easily imagine the cold even on a warm day. Ice was cut in large blocks on the bay in winter, and stored here, packed about with straw. It kept over the summer, no matter how hot the weather. The pit was deep, and it would have been a task indeed to break off pieces and carry them to the dairy with the large iron tongs.

Later in Hamilton's history, ice cutting in winter on the bay for summer use was a means of ready cash for immigrants. Ice cutting in winter on Hamilton Harbour was a major occupation for the working-class residents of the city's poorer north end well into the nineteenth century — until the arrival of electric refrigeration. In this early period, it is likely that MacNab's own staff cut the ice for Dundurn, standing off the shore of MacNab's lower land. Later, when the railroad promoted by Sir Allan cut the bay off, the household probably purchased its ice from dealers.

Food containers in the dairy

The Laundry and Wood Storage Room

The laundry is a large, well-lit room where linens and clothes were cleaned, dried, and pressed. There is a complex of drying racks, presses, rollers, and solid, heavy irons, which were heated before use. The older-style irons are very heavy, and were placed on the room's stove to heat. The newer-style iron had a removable iron core that was heated and then placed back inside the iron. The laundry maid was one of the few servants to be hired outside, and paid on a "per-piece" basis, and was regarded as a specialist. Laundry was quite complex given the many pieces of both male and female attire then. She came in usually three days a week to wash, dry, and press family clothing. This, the far end of the service wing, or west wing, of the house is older than the east. At one end of the laundry are the remains of a powder storage room from the War of 1812 — part of Richard Beasley's house. Beasley used this as his fur store vault. By MacNab's time it was used to store firewood. This section is reached by a Beasley-era tunnel off the kitchen.

Laundry room

Larders and the Cook's Bedroom

Heading back towards the east end of the basement, past the kitchen again, the south passage contains the cook's bedroom — like the butler's upstairs, strategically located near her work in the kitchen and the larders and other small storerooms further along the passageway. Like Wellington's room upstairs, Old Anne's room is small, but clean and cozy. Having her own room and its closeness to her work were signs of her position in the household, as the chief female servant, second in order only to Wellington the butler. This passage ends at the servants' hall. Her room is comfortable-looking, but lacks the window that the butler enjoyed on the main floor. There were two passageways, north and south, with the storerooms in the middle. These storerooms included a room for wine, drunk only by adult family members and guests, a room to store travelling chests (the luggage of the day), larders for preserved food (stored in glass jars), and a room where the youngest male servant performed his tasks of sharpening knives and cleaning candlesticks.

Knife sharpener

The cook's room

The Servants' Hall

The servants' hall is surprisingly bright for a basement room. It has large windows looking south and a cozy, comfortable air. Here servants could relax and take their meals and occasional breaks from work — subject only to the immediate hierarchy of cook and butler. The room was kept warm in winter with a large fireplace, and in summer the windows let in fresh air as well as light. At one end are two small bedrooms for female servants. Males were kept safely distant in rooms over the stables outside the house. It is unknown for certain how large the staff was — perhaps a dozen, though the small size of the bedrooms at the end indicates some came in from Hamilton and area to work for the day, returning home each evening.

Servants' table

The Vault and the Well Room

Due north of the servants' hall is the well room. The well room was so called because it contained access to an underground cistern, where rainwater was collected through a system of pipes leading to the roof for use in the house, generally for washing, not drinking, unless the water had been transformed into ale. This room also functioned as a place for produce from the Dundurn farm to be sorted and prepared before being taken to the kitchen or brewery. The room contained a bricked-in stove, used to heat water that was carried to the hip bath in Aunt Sophia's bedroom.

A small room just off the well room to the north (and sitting directly under Lady MacNab's boudoir) was used as a vault for Sir Allan's business papers, kept in strong boxes to protect them from fire or other damage. Here were the deeds and mortgages that formed the foundation of his complex web of businesses and land holdings, as well as personal legal papers. The papers were carefully sealed in clearly labelled heavy metal boxes.

Desk in vault with MacNab's business papers

Well room with access to cistern

The Castle Grounds and Gardens

It is a neat edifice, built so as to resemble cut stone, and has a very imposing appearance. In front of the castle are numerous gravel walks and an umbrageoud shrubbery, which forms a cool retreat from the scorching rays of the sun. To the southern extremity, facing the city, is a spacious park, surrounded by maple and poplar trees, with a carriage road through the centre. Twining in the direction of the bay, we suddenly come upon the family burial place, where rests many a brave veteran.... A few hundred yards northward from the castle, a view will there be obtained surpassing anything I have ever seen. The

Above: The Rolph gates
Opposite page: Back facade, facing grounds and the bay

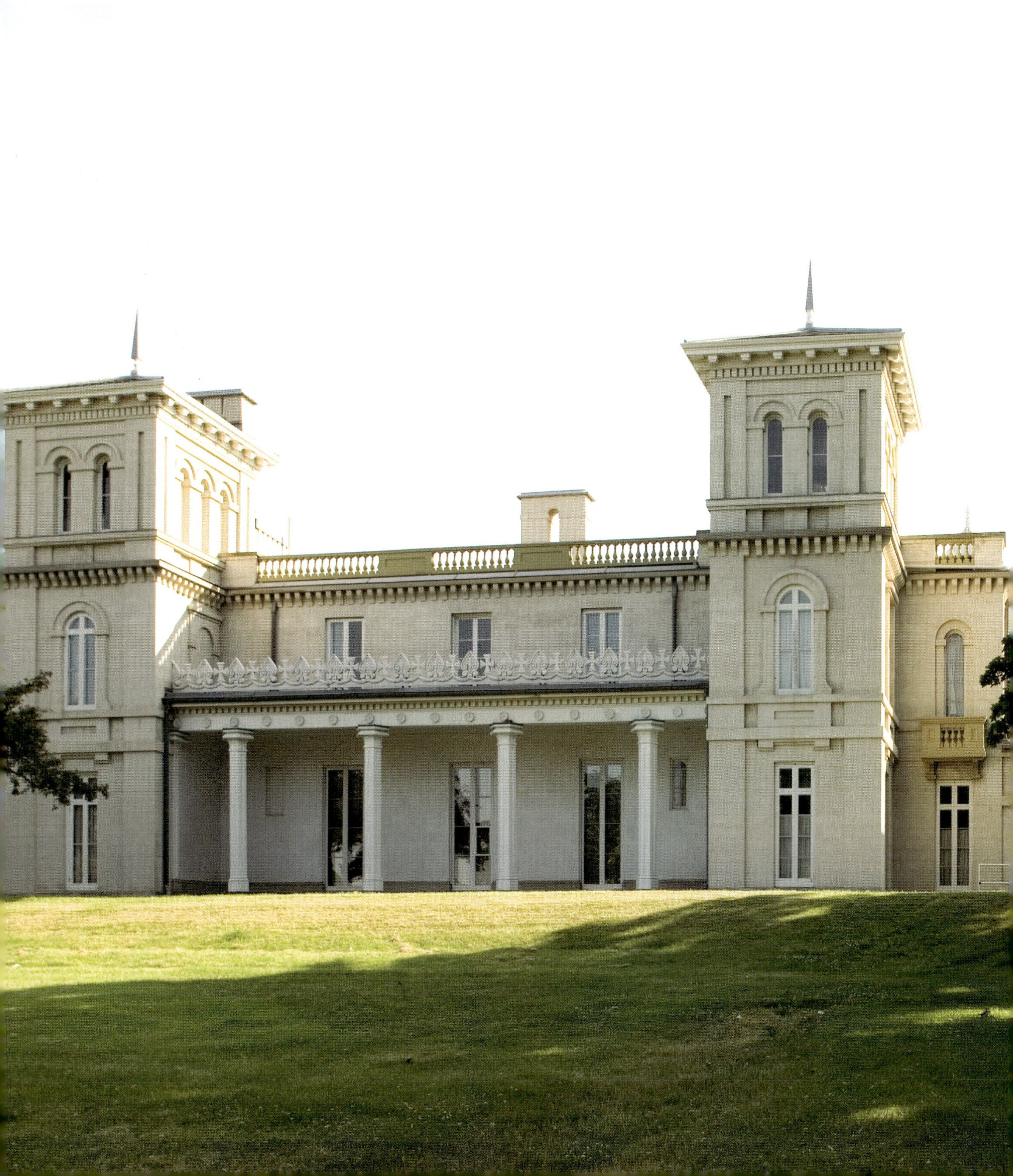

The cockpit

> bay, smooth as a mirror, and blue as the heavens above it.
> — Hamilton Spectator, *July 20, 1846*

Dundurn Castle has had modifications during its long life (including a major renovation in 1847 of the interior, the roof, and the outbuildings), but none that has changed the overall feeling this house projects to the passerby. This passage was written soon after the death of Allan MacNab's second wife, Mary, but could describe the scene today.

The grounds were planned so that lodges and gates could be erected marking its territory. These were not all built immediately, but two were to appear over time. Battery Lodge exists still as the principal gatehouse to the castle. For a time in 1846, the schoolmaster who taught Sophia and

Dovecote at the west end of Dundurn

Minnie at Dundurn lived there. Later a second small house, called Castle Douane, or Dean, was erected on the grounds to the east. It still exists as a private house, though with an addition dating from the early twentieth century.

In 1846, perhaps to divert his attention away from his dying wife, Sir Allan had a fence built, with a hedge planted along its length, and extended the road — probably York Street — so it would connect with his circular drive. He had roses, shrubs, and willow trees planted along the road. Sir Allan employed a landscape gardener, William Reid, for his grounds. One of the first results was a rose garden near Inchbuie — the family burial plot on the grounds — and a taming of Beasley's orchard. To keep his younger daughters busy with a happier distraction while their mother was ill, he had Reid show them how to plant their own garden plots. There was a kitchen garden also, which is now restored as part of the ongoing life of Dundurn today.

The most mysterious and interesting building is located to the northeast — the cockpit. This building resembles a Grecian temple and is thought to have been built to allow Regency gentlemen of Hamilton to engage in the eighteenth century "sport" of cock fighting, with the betting that provided the real pleasure. It seems it was never used for this purpose and merely provided something picturesque for the estate, a kind of Italianate folly. The folly was a neo-Gothic architectural whimsy that placed manufactured romantic ruins in the gardens of great houses.

Another unusual feature is the dovecote Sir Allan had designed and built at the west end of Dundurn. Dovecotes (or doocotes as they were called in Scotland) were a sign of the aristocracy across western Europe. They sheltered and nurtured doves, but actually at Dundurn, mostly pigeons, which were kept for their eggs, meat, and droppings (used as fertilizer). But for Allan MacNab, the dovecote was mostly a sign of his status as Laird of his New World Dundurn — though there is some evidence it was used for its original purpose. By the nineteenth century when Dundurn was designed and built, dovecotes were already falling out of fashion in Scotland for practical purposes as sources of eggs and fowl. It was on the dovecote that MacNab placed the family crest, displaying the severed head of the rival MacNeish clan.

Stable area

The coach house, with the male servants' quarters, is architecturally quite different from the main house. It is of rough stonework— not rubble stone, but crudely dressed stone — and similar to Loyalist Gothic-Revival styles more typical of later in the century, with its peaked roof adornment over the central doors. The stables were enlarged in 1847.

Missing entirely from today's Dundurn is the MacNab family burial place, named Inchbuie after the traditional burying ground for the Clan MacNab in Scotland. It was located on the grounds to the east looking out over the bay, and surrounded by its own stone wall. Here was buried MacNab's only son, Robert, killed in a hunting accident at the age of eleven in 1834, before the house was complete. MacNab's first wife, Elizabeth Brooke, then his second, Lady Mary, were buried here, as well as his parents, removed from their graves in Toronto. Long after his own death, the family was divided, the bodies disinterred and moved to two separate cemeteries — Hamilton for the Protestants, and Holy Sepulchre for the Catholics, Sir Allan included among the Catholics. The Canadian Inchbuie has now vanished although its location is marked. The original Inchbuie is an island near Loch Tay which still contains the graves of fifteen chiefs of Clan MacNab.

Part II

THE LIFE OF SIR ALLAN MACNAB

At 8 o'clock we set out in a Boat to go to Beasley at the head of Burlington Bay about 8 miles. The River & Bay were full of Canoes, the Indians were fishing, we bought some fine Salmon of them. When we had crossed the Bay Beasly house became a very pretty object. We landed at it & walked up the hill from whence is a beautiful view of the Lake with Wooded Points breaking the line of Shore & Flamborough head in the background. The hill is quite like a park, fine turf with large Oak trees dispersed but no underwood.... The country appears more fitt for the reception of Inhabitants than any part of the Province I have seen.
—Elizabeth Simcoe, June 11, 1796

Beasley Hollow, Hamilton, by John Herbert Caddy (1801–1887)

Today the height of land at the very western end of Lake Ontario still presents a beautiful sight to those fortunate enough to see it from the water. One still sees mostly trees, and another "very pretty object" standing on the spot where Beasley's house stood more than two hundred years ago. If one overlooks the rail lines visible at its foot, it is easy to imagine the time before the arrival of Elizabeth Simcoe's inhabitants.

Before this house, and before the rail lines and the city were built, this was a land of trees, grasses, wildlife, and an old culture of people living with the land. Amerindian trails crossed the heights, a natural avenue to travel around the lake and down towards the great falls at Niagara and back. The Europeans called the people who hunted and fished for salmon in the pure waters of the bay the Mississauga.

With the end of the American Revolutionary War, Americans loyal to the Crown settled first in Upper Canada on the Niagara River near the falls. From there, they moved gradually up towards the head of the lake. Much of their economic activity was centred on trading furs with the Mississauga. Richard Beasley, the most important of these "Indian traders," arrived in 1779, and built a log cabin by the shore near his wharf and fur warehouses. He prospered as a trader and a dozen years later was able to build a brick house with outbuildings on the heights above. Under the main house, Beasley dug storage cellars, perhaps for furs and other goods. As Simcoe described it, the property was park-like, with two hundred apple trees, a tree nursery, other fruit trees, in particular peach, an ice house, a smokehouse to prepare his own meat, and a wash house.

This Beasley house was commandeered by the military during the War of 1812, and he and his family had to move back into their log house for a time. The soldiers dug up the grounds to build defensive ramparts, and damaged the house during their occupation. After the war, Beasley did recover, and again prospered. In 1832, he decided to move into the growing village of Hamilton and sold the property to a Kingston cousin named John Solomon Cartwright. Later that year, Cartwright sold the 1,100 acres on Burlington Heights for the then spectacular sum of £2,500.

The purchaser, Allan Napier MacNab, a young lawyer and entrepreneur, was Cartwright's business partner, a man who had strutted into town just six years earlier, determined to make his mark in the fast-growing community. This property, and the fine house he would build upon it, would ensure his mark remained visible in Hamilton for generations to come. His inspiration for this landmark lay in his own past, in the Highlands of Scotland with clan MacNab.

War of 1812 era flintlock pistol

Early Life and Character

A severed head and the motto "Let fear be far from all," *timor omnis abesto*, adorn the family crest of the highland Scots MacNab clan. On February 19, 1798, in the capital of the new British colony of Upper Canada, a lusty baby boy, Allan Napier MacNab, was born into this martial family during an era of war. He would live up to the clan motto all his life.

The MacNabs' ancestral home was a place called Dundurn on Loch Earn, west of Perth in the Highlands. A beautiful, if impoverished, place in the eighteenth century, looking not unlike the west end of Lake Ontario, it supplied soldiers for the British army. The MacNab clan has a long and violent history in the Highlands. The real severed head was garnered in 1612 after a raid on the fastness of the rival MacNeishes. The MacNabs brought home with them a gory trophy, the head of the chief of the clan MacNeish. Allan MacNab's grandfather was leader of a cadet branch of the MacNab clan. Their home, whose name in Scottish Gaelic

The head of Lake Ontario, watercolour over pencil, 1796, by Elizabeth Simcoe (1766–1850)

Courthouse and jail, York, 1829, watercolour by James Pattison Cockburn

means "fort or hill on the water," was likely just a small, fortified house on a height of land, the usual pattern for the heart of the Highlands. Nonetheless, it was a proud emblem in the family's history and imagination. Allan Napier, third child born to his parents and the first to survive of this generation of the MacNabs, imbibed his family's history with pride from the beginning.

The family's martial tradition lived on in Allan Napier MacNab's father, also named Allan, a military man living in an era of what we would call world war. Napoleon and Britain were locked in a great, wide-ranging battle: Napoleon for a domination of the global order not seen for centuries, and Britain, although a major power, for survival. In North America, the United States had finished its successful war of nationhood against Britain, leaving the two at peace, if not in perfect harmony. The infant MacNab's father entered the British army as a junior officer in the 71st Regiment, a unit composed of Highlanders and raised in 1758. Allan senior was promoted to lieutenant and posted to North America to fight in the Revolutionary War as a member of the Queen's Rangers. The Rangers, under the command of Lt. Col. John Graves Simcoe, the man who would later be given the responsibility of founding the new colony of Upper Canada, had been raised in 1776, a mix of American Loyalists and Highland Scots.

At the end of the Revolutionary War, the regiment was disbanded and Lieutenant MacNab was placed on half-pay, the usual practice for redundant officers in the British army in those days. Rather than returning to his native Highlands, never the richest place on earth, Allan MacNab senior moved to the British North American capital at Quebec, where he met and married Anne Napier. He was here when the news came that his old commander Simcoe had been appointed lieutenant-governor of the new colony. Simcoe was a man in a hurry, needing to set up the basic structures of governance and law very quickly as the refugees flooded into what were formerly the western reaches of Quebec (up the St. Lawrence, and therefore named Upper Canada).

In those days, place and advancement in society were attained through personal connections and favours — one expected to be cared for by those immediately above in the social hierarchy. For people in MacNab's position — on the lower rung of the upper class, "the right kind of people" but without wealth or position — Canada was a place that offered the chance to move up the social scale, a difficult and almost impossible task in Britain. MacNab and his fellows were not interested in overthrowing the system, as the Americans had just begun to do, but in replicating it in North America, with themselves playing the role of squire. Allan MacNab senior, the boy from the Gaelic Highlands, was literate, and thus a gentleman, and he hurried to see what opportunities might be available through Simcoe. However, by the time MacNab reached the small capital at Newark, there were few places left, although Simcoe did make him his aide-de-camp, and then a government clerk.

Despite the jobs he was given and despite his

Portrait of MacNab's father hanging in MacNab's dressing room

half-pay officer's salary, Allan MacNab senior soon went into debt. Not long after the birth of Allan junior, he found himself in jail in York for debt. Apparently the door was only lightly secured, as he merely walked away after a few days. He left for Halifax, the military centre of British North America, hoping for a regular officer's commission in the army, again from his patron Simcoe, who had moved on in the imperial service to the West Indies. He met with no luck, but word came from the Loyalist leader William Jarvis in 1802 that a position had been found for him in the government in York. MacNab raised the money to take his family back to Upper Canada, only to find when he got there that the position had evaporated. He was forced to remain in York, as he had spent all his money travelling. MacNab found work and was able to rent a comfortable home for his young family on

Fort George, Niagara, 1812, watercolour and ink by Alfred Sandham (1838–1910)

King Street near the Don River. By 1805, they were even able to employ a servant.

Allan junior spent his boyhood in the growing provincial capital with his parents, and eventually a total of three younger sisters and a much younger brother. MacNab was taught by a local schoolmaster, then later attended the Home District Grammar School, founded by John Strachan to teach the children of the colony's elite families. At school Allan learned the value and necessity of personal contacts and the use of his bare knuckles, delighting in playground skirmishes as much as in wild fun, affinities that would serve him well in his adult years in the politics of a colonial society. MacNab loved this society from an early age, but even as a schoolboy he recognized that his father, while respected by the local elite, was never quite a full member. He had the proper pedigree because of his family connection to the clan leadership, but never the money. The clan MacNab was itself never one of the richest Highland clans either. He resolved to move not only himself but his clan in Canada to a higher plane.

The War of 1812 was young Allan's first opportunity to make his mark. In 1813, a force of 1,700 Americans attacked the capital, York. Although only fifteen years old, MacNab joined in the battle. He was not injured in this defeat, and accompanied the retreating defending force to Kingston, where he joined the provincial navy on the Great Lakes for a short time, and saw battle at Sacketts Harbour. He apparently didn't care for the navy life, and moved on to the Niagara area. There he joined the British regular forces' 100th Regiment, and was involved in heavy fighting when the British forces captured the American Fort Niagara, Buffalo, and the land between in 1813. As a reward for his "bravery and zeal," he received a commission as a junior officer with the 49th Regiment of regulars, stationed at Montreal. The young ensign took part in the campaign into the United States to Plattsburgh, where he commanded an advance force in heavy fighting. But, again the British army retreated. Despite being the largest army assembled by the British in this war, its commander, Sir George Prevost, was timid, and feared the Americans had even greater numbers. In utter frustration, MacNab broke his sword over his knee. By 1814, the regiment was reduced and MacNab put on half pay, a seasoned veteran at the tender age of sixteen. He became known as the "boy hero" of the War of 1812 for his many exploits.

He decamped to York, where family connections brought him a place studying law with the provincial attorney general, D'Arcy Boulton. His father was in dire financial straits again, all the family furniture having been sold to pay debts. MacNab junior was a poor student in both senses of the word, still hoping over the next few years for a full commission in the army, preferring the active life of a soldier to more intellectual pursuits. But the law was desirable as a gentleman's calling, and Boulton represented the very pinnacle of colonial society in Upper Canada — the leading family of the now infamous Family Compact. These were a group of leading politicians, businessmen, and clergy who believed in aristocratic rule by themselves, and who were often in this little colonial world related by marriage. MacNab held other jobs while he was studying — he was a clerk for the legislature, and an inspector of flour, pork, and pot and pearl ashes — which is to say, his connections

Above: George IV (as Prince Regent), enamel on copper, by Henry Bone (1755–1834), principal painter to the prince in 1815
Inset: Sword at the Hamilton Military Museum

A portrait of Sir Isaac Brock, by Theodore George Berthon, painted in 1883

got him government work, the only kind of work that paid real cash on anything like a regular basis. Other jobs he held were not so lofty: carpenter, peddler, miller, and distiller. He amused himself (and thereby risked his social standing) by acting in amateur theatre. And during these years he became well known about the little town of York, drawing comment for his "handsome" form and imposing physique as he strode confidently about, his charismatic personality winning him friends and supporters even as he struggled to find his professional and financial footing, as his fortunes followed a financial roller-coaster ride.

On May 6, 1821, Allan Napier MacNab married Elizabeth Brooke, whose father was also a retired regular army lieutenant on half-pay. MacNab seemed prosperous; he built a comfortable house on King Street that even had the modern convenience of running water in the kitchen. The couple's first child, Robert Allan, was born in 1823, and was followed by two girls, Anne Jane in 1825 and Elizabeth Brooke in early 1826. But by that year MacNab faced serious financial difficulties. His business at the time, a mill, had failed, and another venture, the promotion of Dundurn village, located just south and west of modern Thornhill, came to nothing. That endeavour, entered jointly with the Boulton and Brooke families in 1825, was his first, and unsuccessful, Dundurn in the new world.

The year 1826 was pivotal for Allan MacNab. He again tried for a full-pay commission in the army, hoping to repair his financial situation. His finances were so fragile he could not afford to purchase a uniform, and was snubbed by the regiment he hoped to join in Kingston. But worse yet, his wife, Elizabeth, died in November, leaving him with young children to raise. His elderly parents were increasingly infirm and had begun to lean heavily on him for support. Yet there was a glimmer of light within this dark period. He was admitted to the bar of the Law Society of Upper Canada and could finally hang out his shingle as a qualified lawyer. More fatefully, he made the decision to leave behind the problems and defeats of his boyhood home and go west to seek his fortune, to the growing village of Hamilton, some forty miles away by corduroy and dirt road — a journey of several hours in those days.

A Canadian Dundurn

With a wealth of experience, if not hard cash, and newly minted as a lawyer, MacNab arrived in Hamilton to set up practice. Now twenty-eight years old, the newcomer was immediately noticed. Like his father, he was a powerfully built man, dark-haired, taller than average, the image of a fierce Highland Scot. Though not conventionally handsome, he had a large supply of that immeasurable but invaluable quality called charisma. It was his air, an aura of confidence, of a man going places, that said here was a man to watch, and to follow. His new clients found him both brisk and sympathetic, an unlikely combination that made others trust him with their legal affairs.

The fortune Allan MacNab began to accumulate over the next few years in Hamilton was

Hamilton from the Mountain Road, drawing by L. Young, lithography by Saxony & Major, New York, pre-1850

Bank of Upper Canada, Hamilton branch, at James and Vine streets, 1850s

founded on his law practice, though in spite of his admission to the bar, he knew little law. Donald Beer, his biographer, notes that MacNab himself said he was more fond of fishing and shooting than of reading law. Rather, he was a barrister — a courtroom performer — who won cases with force of personality. He easily translated his boyhood schoolyard combative spirit to the courtroom, where his skill with words knocked his opponents down and out. From the money he earned with his increasingly popular practice, he began to speculate in land.

Land was the one commodity Upper Canada had in surplus. Hamilton itself was planned and built by land speculators, who managed to have it declared the district seat of the new district of Gore that was formed after the war, and thus home to the local court system. No doubt the ready availability of land had attracted MacNab to the village. He was not the first lawyer there, but quickly became the most active and important.

Land was purchased with cash or debt; land was leased, or rented, or sold on promises to pay from the purchaser. In those days entrepreneurs such as MacNab relied on a range of means to secure financing. There was one early bank, centred in Toronto, the Bank of Upper Canada, controlled by the York elite, for those times when cash was indispensable. More often MacNab drew on mortgages on property; personal loans from individuals, both friends and family; stocks; and promissory notes.

MacNab used credit as creatively as possible. There was little actual cash in the colony for quite some time, and no regular, regulated currency for much of the nineteenth century. A complex economic system based on land development, where mortgages were more important than cash, grew in the village and in the province. In such a situation, one's reputation was all. Business used a system of barter, supplemented with cash, but more often with promises to pay, based on personal acquaintance.

The middle classes and the aristocracy were expected to show their position in the world in a tangible way — primarily through their houses, but also in their schooling, dress, friends, and personal habits of display. Society was based from top to bottom on relationships of a client-patron nature and on a display proper to one's status — whatever the reality of colonial economics. Allan Napier MacNab fit this society exactly.

In the village, MacNab wasted no time in establishing an entrepreneurial presence. He immediately began to build and sell or rent houses, stores, offices, warehouses, a tavern. Hamilton was a growing commercial centre:

industry was still decades away for this entrepreneurial place. Farmers from the United States and from Britain were pouring into the western reaches of Upper Canada, where lay the best agricultural land. Farmers needed goods to set up, tools to clear land, seed, iron stoves, and so on. In 1823, before MacNab's arrival, the local leadership had prevailed on the colonial government to dig a canal through the beach strip, which both protected and isolated the harbour from Lake Ontario, to help transport goods to the new settlements. From the beginning, this canal was to receive government funding for improvements. Hamilton's bay shore was the first and easiest landfall for the goods that began to come through the canal.

Hamilton courthouse as it looked from 1832 to 1879, drawing by Marcus Smith in 1850–1851

The earliest businesses in Hamilton were thus private wharfs and warehouses lining Hamilton's shoreline due north of the village centre. With the construction of a courthouse in the mid-1820s, Hamilton began to boom. Its lots had been carefully laid out by the original developers such that they would easily accommodate a mix of stores, commercial properties, houses, and other establishments in an equitable fashion. It is no wonder that Allan MacNab saw a good future waiting for him here, away from York where all the best prospects for advancement were already long held by elite families. Within just a few months of his arrival in Hamilton, MacNab was one of the leading citizens present to welcome the colony's lieutenant-governor for the official opening of the canal.

In 1832, a new stone courthouse was constructed to replace the wood structure of the 1820s, and Allan MacNab moved his by now very successful law practice there. The 1830s were especially prosperous, both for the village and for MacNab. In 1831, land prices in Hamilton had tripled since his arrival, adding to his growing wealth. His timing had been exactly right.

From the outset, MacNab was never above some shady practices — sometimes using clients' money without their knowledge, and in one case apparently selling the same plot of land to three different people. This seems incredible to us today, in our world of Enrons and other corporate scandals. Yet, in these early days, land was often not yet surveyed, and title was difficult to ascertain. As few paid in cash, it is possible MacNab had not received payment for the earlier sales, so sold again to someone more promising. But it is difficult to tell what actually happened in these chaotic times — only that MacNab could be ruthless when necessary. Yet, throughout it all, his reputation for personal integrity was unassailed, even by enemies. People trusted him. Even the man who would be his greatest enemy, William Mackenzie, recognized his personal qualities, principally his honour and his word, referring to MacNab's "disinterested integrity" in business dealings. It did not hurt either, that MacNab had fought in the War of 1812, or that his father fought in the Revolutionary War. Most of the elite of the little village of Hamilton shared these experiences, which gave him an entree into society.

Soon after he came to Hamilton, MacNab also got involved politically. Politics was a raw, rough game then, played in the courts, the legislature, throughout election campaigns, and sometimes violently in public. Not long after his arrival, a number of men in disguise, among whom might have been MacNab, as alleged by his enemies, had tarred and feathered a prominent local reformer, George Rolph, guilty, they alleged, of living in adultery with his married servant and housekeeper. More importantly, however, Rolph was a leader of the reform faction that wanted to end the control of the Family Compact over colonial society. Rolph brought a civil case for damages, as the government refused to prosecute or even investigate. The attorney-general's son, and now solicitor-general of the colony acting privately, Henry John Boulton was assisted by MacNab and another lawyer as counsel. This was a political case at its heart, as elections were coming up and Rolph's case was argued by the Baldwins, William Warren and Robert, the even more prominent reformers, and by Rolph's brother Dr. John. Rolph was unsuccessful with the civil suit, so he brought charges privately against the eight Tory defendants at Quarter Sessions, the criminal court. This time MacNab was one of the defendants. MacNab conducted his own case. He did so with such force that many began to suspect he had political aspirations. He had begun to make his name as a Tory to be contended with in the Gore District.

His next opportunity to make his name politically came in 1829. At the end of January, the new lieutenant-governor, Sir John Colborne, was hung in effigy in Hamilton by parties unknown, though MacNab was suspected to be among the perpetrators. This incident, called "The Hamilton Outrage," became an issue in the legislature, and Allan MacNab was called as a witness before a select committee, headed by two members of the Reform Party, W.W. Baldwin and John Rolph, the brother of George of the tarring-and-feathering case. MacNab appeared twice, and was happily combative. The Reform-dominated committee then presented a report to the legislature on MacNab's refusal to answer direct questions. He was ordered to present himself to the House to explain why he had refused to answer questions, and to stand accused of breaching the privileges of the legislature. MacNab performed even more happily before the House, denying their right to question him, or to charge him. Always one to enjoy a good fight, he used his verbal fists with no holding back, accusing his opponents of "low cunning" and of being fools, liars, and asses. By a majority vote, he was sentenced to jail for contempt. His supporters played the event up as much as possible for the political theatre that it was. After ten days, MacNab wrote a conciliatory letter to the Speaker of the Legislature and the issue blew over.

It was something of a tempest in a teapot even in Hamilton. But his defiant actions, and then his conciliatory tone at just the right point, marked him as a political player, increasing his prominence in the Gore District, and in Hamilton especially. He was now becoming a leading, if not *the* leading, character of the village and district. MacNab, as a direct result of this growing prominence and his ability to sell himself, successfully entered into formal politics in the 1830 general election, winning a seat as one of the two members for Wentworth County.

MacNab invested in other developments, one of which, the Desjardins Canal project, reflected his importance as an entrepreneur and investor. The project was an attempt by some Dundas merchants to forestall the growth of Hamilton as a trans-shipment centre by allowing shipping to move from the harbour into Dundas. Dundas was separated from the harbour proper by Burlington Heights and a swamp to the west of that, but was at this time a centre of early indus-

A proclamation and lecture notice by William Lyon Mackenzie

try. A canal was planned through the swamp, and initiated by deepening a small natural outlet at the northern end of the heights. A company had been formed to promote the canal in 1826, and MacNab joined it as his personal projects began to bring him a degree of wealth. By 1830, the project was moribund when MacNab gained control of the company, which he tightened over the next two years. There never seemed to be enough money. Originally envisioned as a barge canal, MacNab insisted it be dug deep enough to admit lake ships directly. He was correct, of course, that this was needed to make the project successful — but the engineering difficulties and constant shortage of funds to overcome them worked against the project's success.

At the same time, he entered into another canal and river project to connect Lake Erie to Brantford using the Grand River. Its purpose was to draw

Christ's Church Cathedral, Hamilton, circa 1848, by F.M. Bell Smith (1846–1923)

was hedging his bets.

Another project, more closely related to the fortunes of Hamilton, and therefore to MacNab, was a plan to launch the steamboat *Constitution*, at an estimated cost of £6,000. A syndicate of investors was organized to raise the capital in the form of stocks and cash. MacNab was involved to the point of advancing much of the money himself. The steamer was ready in 1834, and sailed between Hamilton, York, and Niagara.

MacNab was taking his place in the community in ways other than his politics and business. He was a warden of St. John's Church of England parish in Ancaster, and later was a leading figure in promoting the building of Christ's Church in Hamilton. There was a long tradition in England of adherence to the Church of England as a necessary

trade *away* from Dundas and the Desjardins Canal. This project never amounted to much, and MacNab was not heavily involved, except in a legal capacity. All the same, it is puzzling he would be involved in competing against himself, unless he route to social and political prominence, and although the Church of England was never quite to acquire the same status across the pond as it held in England, it was still regarded informally as *the* church of empire. Socially prominent people were Anglicans, whatever their private beliefs (or lack of same) might be. He also got involved in the military again, becoming second-in-command of the 4th Gore Militia regiment in 1830 with the rank of lieutenant colonel.

The headiness of these early years in Hamilton was tempered by the loss of his mother in 1828, and of his father, Allan senior, in 1830. The family gradually gathered about him in Hamilton as its new head. MacNab's immediate household consisting of his two young children, Robert Allan and Anne Jane, and his three younger sisters who had come with him in 1826, settled in a house on James Street. His younger brother David followed later, to also set up in business in the village.

In 1831, ten years after his first nuptials, Allan MacNab remarried, to Mary Stuart of Brockville. Although she was a Roman Catholic — MacNab was an Anglican — her blood was a colonial blue, being related to the Anglican Stuarts of Kingston and the Boultons of York, both family stalwarts of the Family Compact. Mary was to be a sensible influence on his life, but also through her network of family connections brought a more aristocratic note into the home than had Elizabeth Brooke. MacNab was steadily moving up the social ladder. Mary's family had come to York after the death of her father, the sheriff of Johnstown District in the eastern part of Upper Canada; MacNab must have met her in York while the legislature was sitting. When they married, MacNab was thirty-two and Mary a young woman of nineteen. Their age difference, and MacNab's growing importance, no doubt made the match attractive in the eyes of the widowed mother of the bride. Over the next few years, MacNab and Mary had two children, Sophia and Mary Stuart, called Minnie, His household must have been lively with these two young girls, and his son, Robert, and daughter Anne Jane from his first marriage.

Allan MacNab had lived in Hamilton only six

Young Sophia MacNab, late 1830s, painting attributed to Robert Whale

years. He had come with just a few dollars in his pocket, with children and sisters to support, and the grief over a recently deceased and loved wife. But he had two important assets: his new status as barrister and his exuberant confidence. By the end of 1832, he was a member of the legislature, a major land owner, the most important lawyer in the district, a warden of the Church of England, and a successful entrepreneur in a growing community. He was well connected to the colony's elite Tory families — and once again happily married. Allan Napier MacNab was now poised to mark his full membership in an informal colonial aristocracy with a house proper to that status — a house that not only reflected his image, but reinforced it and made his place in society real. MacNab had used the name Dundurn once before in the abortive settlement near Thornhill, before he gave up on York and moved to

Hamilton. This time, he would build a proper Dundurn, the home of a laird in a new Scotland.

On November 16, 1832, a fire ravaged the central district of Hamilton village, destroying many of Allan's and his brother David's properties, and damaging Allan's own home. On that same date, MacNab paid, or promised to pay, £2,500 for the former Beasley property, now owned by John Solomon Cartwright of Kingston, on Burlington Heights. Here was the perfect locale for a Canadian Dundurn, to be better than the old and truly reflective of its owner's ranking in society.

Robert Charles Wetherell, an English-trained architect, had just opened for business in Hamilton. MacNab hired him to design Dundurn, which would be his greatest project. For Dundurn, he chose an Italianate style. MacNab mostly left Wetherell alone to do his work, except to insist that something of the Beasley house be incorporated into the new. The only other request was to place the grisly MacNab crest on the dovecote. MacNab also expended money and debt on a landscaper to perfect that designed wildness that was coming to define the English garden, a reaction to the ordered gardens of the eighteenth century.

What does Dundurn say? The house says that Allan Napier MacNab could not conceive in terms other than large, that his vision was slightly ahead of the times, though his feet were firmly placed on the foundations of history. He was a man who looked ahead, rather than back, choosing the latest, not yet popular architectural style for a home that would be a work-in-progress for the rest of his life. The house says too that he saw a Hamilton, and a Canada, that did not yet exist but would — a place of prosperity and greatness, rather than the small, utilitarian settlements that were his everyday reality. The house spoke of a society founded on its roots: he insisted that part of Richard Beasley's house remain in the foundations of Dundurn. It looked, as it always had, over the bay below, but later was also to look down at MacNab's railroad, just as Richard Beasley's house had watched his wharf and fur warehouses. The house also expressed MacNab's belief in an ordered society — of servants who were not employees, but persons proper to that order — and of masters and mistresses also born to that order. It was designed to fit neatly into its working orchard, and to be surrounded by a nature tamed to look wild.

The family and staff that populated the house changed as well over the years. The greatest loss came in 1834, when MacNab's son, Robert, only eleven, fatally shot himself in a hunting accident while MacNab was away on his new ship *Constitution*. He was buried in Inchbuie, the private cemetery MacNab set on the northeastern part of the property, overlooking the bay. MacNab decided then to move his parents to this place, keeping the family together in their Canadian Dundurn.

MacNab's political position during the 1830s cannot easily be detached from his financial dealings — though there were points of departure. In the legislature, he resolutely opposed reform and supported the hierarchical Tory vision of Upper Canada. He was involved in the five expulsions of William Lyon Mackenzie from the legislature in the early 1830s, perhaps also smarting to some extent over Mackenzie's involvement as one of the prosecutors in the "Hamilton Outrage" incident. He built a reputation in the legislature for hard and careful work in committees and in preparing bills that counterbalanced his public antics. There was a time for performance and a time for work, and MacNab was intelligent enough to know the difference.

He did not cross a certain line that would have meant insult to the financial leadership of York either. The colony's premier bank, the Bank of Upper Canada, had extended long credit to him

Boathouses at MacKay's wharf, Hamilton Harbour, from the Canadian Illustrated News, *February 13, 1864*

to help finance his many entangled business deals and land holdings. In return for his support in the legislature, they appointed him their solicitor for the Gore District. He did, however, support where he could the rival Commercial Bank, located in Kingston. This careful behind-the-scenes, involvement in banking was necessary, as the value of his holdings fluctuated frequently — without even considering the disastrous fire of 1832 and the cost of purchasing the Beasley/Cartwright property on the heights. In 1834, he lost his position with the Desjardins Canal company, though this was not an unmitigated disaster given the even shakier position of that company's finances. The year before, the colony's government, which is to say the York elite, had taken control over land development in the colony. MacNab reacted by introducing a bank bill into the legislature. After some problems getting approval, the Gore Bank was chartered provincially in 1835, the very year the seventy-two rooms of Dundurn were ready for habitation.

There is nothing like having your own bank to smooth over financial difficulties and shortfalls. With this new source of funds, there were few obstacles in MacNab's path to financial growth. Just two years later, by 1837, in addition to his land dealings and holdings, he operated a

Boathouse at Hamilton Harbour, 1850s

steamship line on Lake Ontario, owned a dock, and was promoting two railroads. His move into railroads resonates with his choice of architecture for Dundurn. The house revealed a man who was slightly ahead of the times; so too the railroads. George Stephenson in England had demonstrated the technical possibilities of steam-powered railways with his *Rocket* in 1829. The first locomotives in the Hamilton area was contemplated by the village's founder, George Hamilton, in 1832, only three years later. This line, called the London and Gore Railway Company, received a charter in 1834, and listed Allan MacNab among its supporters. Railways, however, were of a different order of financing than speculating in wild lands, or of building sites in small, ambitious villages (though Hamilton became a town officially in 1833). Financing then was beyond the ability even of the provincial government, and eventually required the infusion of British capital.

Oddly, MacNab was in some ways not the "compleat" Tory. He was pragmatic where development was concerned, advocating for increased American immigration, utilizing New York markets where possible, and foreseeing his later railroad projects as means to providing transshipment of American goods and people between New York and Michigan. He saw too, the Toronto Tory Bank of Upper Canada as a roadblock, leading him to found the Gore Bank in Hamilton. The Gore Bank was to outlast the Bank of Upper Canada. MacNab was also socially eclectic. He supported the Clergy Reserves, a flash point in political battling of the day, but believed revenues from their sale should be divided equally among all religious denominations; the proper Tory position was that they belonged to the Church of England only, and should be maintained for its sole support. He was a supporter of the Church of England locally, but had on occasion attended the local Presbyterian Church, and his second wife, Mary Stuart, and their two daughters were Catholic. He was, however, firmly on the Tory side in his opposition to responsible government. Despite his liberal views in many aspects of his life, he was at heart a Regency gentleman, for whom some were destined by breeding and blood to rule, and others to obey, in a complex hierarchical ordering of society.

The year 1837 also saw the first great event held at Dundurn. Allan MacNab's youngest sister, Lucy, married his law partner John Hatt on March 17. Although Mary Stuart MacNab was already showing the early signs of what was probably tuberculosis, she presided over the household celebration. She was helped by her sister, Sophia Stuart, who had come to reinforce the very female household. She was to marry Allan's brother, David Archibald, the next year. In September,

MacNab and John Solomon Cartwright were proclaimed "crown lawyers," the first Queen's Counsels in Canada, Queen Victoria having ascended the throne earlier in the year.

The events of 1837 were to put a brake on his work temporarily, but more importantly upset his Tory vision of the proper ordering of society. His legislative rival, indeed his enemy, William Lyon Mackenzie, headed an armed insurrection against the colony's government and entrenched elites. MacNab rose to fight this threat, this time in a literal sense. Mackenzie, the reformer and publisher of a widely read newspaper, *The Colonial Advocate*, pushed for a greater democratization of Upper Canadian society. At this time, the governor was appointed by the British government and was responsible to them alone. He, himself, appointed his own advisors from members of the local elite, and parliament consisted of two houses, only one of which was elected. MacNab fully supported this aristocratic system, as did his business partners in the colony. Reformers in both Upper and Lower Canada (Quebec) were increasingly frustrated in their attempts to bring about change. Revolution seemed the only answer.

Mackenzie raised the standard of rebellion in December 1837 on Yonge Street north of Toronto. He proposed to march south with his "army" and capture the seat of government. At the same time, a more serious challenge to government was being launched. The governor general of the Canadas resided in Quebec, as the most settled and developed part of British North America outside Halifax. As a result, most of the regular troops and officers in Upper Canada were sent to Lower Canada to deal with the rebellion there. MacNab displayed resolve and a sure sense of the situation, raising sixty-five "Men of the Gore" and rushing them across the lake to Toronto. There Sir Francis Bond Head, the very conservative lieutenant-governor, gave command of the loyal forces to MacNab — whose confident character had impressed the governor — over the adjutant general of militia, Lt. Col. James Fitzgibbon, a retired regular officer. This gentleman's objections soon forced a divided command, though MacNab stayed in real control. With one thousand men, MacNab marched north along Yonge Street, where they met and defeated the rebels in battle at Montgomery's Tavern. Head, over the protests of the remaining regular officers in the colony, then placed MacNab in command of a force sent to deal with another rebel army at London. The campaign was chaotic and ill-led by MacNab in operational terms. The rebel force was defeated, but its leader, Charles Duncombe, a medical doctor, escaped.

Mackenzie was not finished, however. He re-emerged a week later, having occupied Navy Island in the Niagara River between the United States and Upper Canada. On Christmas day, Head sent MacNab in charge of a squad of militia and regular officers to this frontier to deal with Mackenzie. The situation there under MacNab was even more chaotic than at London. Some 3,500 volunteers had gathered by early January to supplement the original force, but nothing much happened. As one historian put it, "MacNab alternated between drilling and dining." In his defence, one can say he had no clear operational orders — whether to attempt to land on Navy Island, or merely to contain Mackenzie there. Things had already become serious at the end of December, while volunteers were still flooding in, when MacNab ordered a contingent to destroy an American ship, the *Caroline*, supplying Mackenzie. In carrying out this order the men killed one of the American crew. This was more typical of MacNab — the brave and grand gesture — than careful military planning. He, no doubt, remembered the retreat from Plattsburgh, when frustration made him break his own sword over

The destruction of the steamboat Caroline, *1837, drawn by G. Tattersall and engraved by J. Harris.*

his knee. Reaction in the United States was belligerent — and MacNab was indicted for murder in Erie County, New York, across the border from Navy Island. The British commander-in-chief in Montreal ordered MacNab replaced by regular officers, and the laird was recalled from his command. Meantime, Mackenzie escaped from the island in the confusion, leaving it empty.

Allan Napier MacNab received honours for these campaigns, which contemporaries applauded, whatever modern historians might think. He was knighted in 1838 for services to the Crown. That winter, the Men of the Gore arrived at Dundurn in sixty-two sleighs where they read an address of approval and thanks to the newly minted knight and his ladies. It seemed now that he had arrived at the pinnacle of his ideal, ordered society — just as this society was to change. He was now a full member of the aristocracy, with house to match, a successful military command behind him, and dealings at every level of business in colonial society. The Canadian Dundurn was truly a seat to be reckoned with. Or, so it seemed, but for the arrival in 1839 in British North America of a British lord with the nickname "Radical Jack." Lord Durham was to issue a famous (or infamous, if you were named Sir Allan MacNab) report, which initiated the end of the Regency world that had formed the knight of Dundurn.

Change in the Air

The 1840s were years that tested Sir Allan MacNab severely, as his social, political, and financial worlds were turned upside down. In trying times, family is often the rock and solace. But deaths in his family added more stress to his life. In 1839, Napier, the young son of his brother David and his sister-in-law, Sophia — the heir to the MacNabs of Dundurn branch of the clan — died and was buried at Inchbuie. A few weeks later, David, the boy's father, who had developed a chest infection in the campaign of 1837, also died and was laid to rest at Inchbuie. Too soon after that, David and Sophia's remaining child, another son, David Archibald, died. Sophia, in deepest mourning, came then to live at Dundurn. These events were capped dreadfully with the death of Sir Allan's wife, Mary, in 1846. Though premature deaths were much more common, people were by no means inured to them, and one can only imagine the grieving this family was experiencing. Yet, life had to go on for the living, and so it did.

The years immediately following the 1837 rebellions were perilous. There were several uprisings and threats of uprisings. MacNab, as a prominent local lawyer, was involved in the prosecutions of the rebels. In some cases he showed great mercy, and even kindness, especially to those who were not leaders. In 1838, Dundurn was put under military guard as a plot was uncovered. A force of two hundred men were to make a diversionary raid on MacNab's home — a fort, indeed, this time — then advance from there on Hamilton jail to release rebel prisoners, and make an escape by steamer from Hamilton Harbour. MacNab made sure the town was filled with militia troops, and the plot was defused without a shot having been fired. Soon after this, a militia captain was assassinated and MacNab learned he

Lord Durham, pastel by Thomas Lawrence (1769–1830)

was next on the hit list. Sir Allan was then heavily involved in forming a permanent militia force of four battalions, with himself heading one. But he was soon pushed out, as the imperial government decided they needed full-time leadership. This move rankled MacNab very much, as he was now entirely out of favour when it came to military matters in the province.

His business affairs were doing little better, despite the higher fees he commanded as a Queen's Counsel, since his attention to military and government matters meant he lost many of his private clients to other lawyers. Land sales, and thus speculation, were in a downturn in this period, too, and rivals forced him off the board of the local Gore Bank. Politically, MacNab was caught in the thick of the changes wrought by the rebellions. In 1839, the imperial government sent Lord Durham to find the root causes of the rebellions and report back. Lord Durham came up with many suggestions for his report from his very brief visit, but few of them pleased Sir Allan. Durham recommended that the Executive Council no longer report to the governor, but be responsible to the elected Assembly. This idea flew in the face of MacNab's sense of the proper ordering of society: it was right that a British society have a parliament where gentlemen debated, but, he held, executive power should remain with the Crown and its advisors, which in British North America meant the governor and his council of appointees, men appointed from the elite, who ruled by inheritance and natural design. Lord Durham also recommended that Upper and Lower Canada be united into one colony called Canada. These changes were put into place in 1840 (though the territory was still divided into Canada East and Canada West) and were to cause much soul-searching for Upper Canadian colonial aristocrats such as MacNab. MacNab was worried, too, that the larger and financially more vibrant Canada East would soon overwhelm the still fragile economy of the smaller Canada West.

By the end of the 1830s, despite his knighthood, MacNab had begun to lose influence. His fees as a Queen's Counsel were scrutinized thoroughly before being granted, and he had no position in the Gore militia. He was out of favour with the new governor, Lord Sydenham, as he had stood for the city of Hamilton and defeated the governor's favourite for that seat in the election. In any case, MacNab did not hold Sydenham in high regard, given his policy of eagerly embracing the new political order. Sydenham froze MacNab out of government preferments, an odd situation for a Tory who idealized the imperial connection and social hierarchy. In some ways the laird of Dundurn was more realistic than the imperial authorities and their representative, Sydenham. He understood that the French would never be assimilated and therefore as long as French and English were thrown together into the same colony, accommodation must be sought for the common good. MacNab was pragmatic in this regard — though he had been a vigorous opponent of responsible government, once it was a *fait accompli* he decided to work with the new system.

In 1840, MacNab's adventure at Navy Island came back to haunt him. One of his supporters, Alexander McLeod, was arrested in Lewiston, New York, and charged with the arson of the *Caroline* and the murder of the American crewman who had died in its sinking. Diplomatic notes crossed the border, but the private opinion of Sydenham was to let the man hang, so long as the British government was out of the matter. This became apparent to MacNab, whose apprehension was magnified by the growing realization his wife was ill with consumption (as tuberculosis was commonly called). MacNab received some relief when, after he testified at McLeod's trial in Utica, New York, a verdict of not guilty was returned. McLeod had, in fact, not been involved in the burning of the ship, although he had been with MacNab's forces in 1837.

Meantime, politically Sir Allan's fortunes went even lower. MacNab travelled to England in 1842 in an attempt to go over the head of Governor Sydenham, but failed utterly, not understanding the new reality, which was the promotion of moderate voices in Canada. He had some followers, but was regarded as too extreme and dated for the new direction. His journey to Britain was, however, fun, MacNab style. Rather than sailing from a Canadian or British North American port, he travelled through the New England states incognito, calling himself either Captain, or Colonel, Johnston. MacNab was still a wanted man for his role in the *Caroline* affair and could have been arrested and tried for murder. In Maine he even met the state governor, no doubt enjoying his reprise of his acting career. All went well and he boarded a British ship at Portland, Maine, for the trip to Liverpool.

He went to visit the original Dundurn, where his father's half-sister took him on a tour of MacNab sites. He also went to present several "addresses" to the Queen at a royal levee. The Colonial Secretary himself presented MacNab, a sign that he was still honoured, if not actually influential. The addresses he carried came from a diverse number of groups: "the coloured popula-

Central Hamilton, near city hall, from an unknown newspaper, circa 1846

tion of Canada," the officers of the militia of the western district, "the Sachems, War Chiefs and Warrior of the Six Nations," the Niagara area, and the Gore District. Clearly, MacNab was popular and trusted among all sorts of people in Canada. He spent time in London being fêted, and looking for funding for his growing railway ventures. Yet, he also had serious issues to address. Politically he pressed for some amelioration of the democracy imposed on the Canadas. Here he failed utterly; the Tory moment had passed. More importantly, he managed to borrow money in the British markets to consolidate and pay off his Canadian debts. Once again, bold brinkmanship paid off for Sir Allan.

Although Sydenham was to die in a riding accident soon after, MacNab was never to regain the sort of personal closeness to the governors of the united Canadas as he had in Upper Canada. He had farther to travel geographically, too, and gout was beginning to test his own physical patience. The capital was at first in Kingston, and then alternated with Montreal, as Kingston was too small. He did make new friends and alliances at

Hamilton, 1853, drawing by Robert Whale

Kingston, the most important being Dominick Daly, the only Catholic member of the legislative council. Sir Charles Bagot succeeded Lord Sydenham as governor general, but died of a heart attack soon after his appointment. Under Bagot, it seemed that full responsible government was in play, as the Executive Council governed as a cabinet, sometimes without reference to the governor.

Bagot's successor, Sir Charles Metcalfe, operated with a kind of benign paternalism, learned in long service in British India. Metcalfe thus created a storm of protest when he refused to sign a bill into law that had passed both houses of the legislature. Metcalfe had instructions from the British government to allow a degree of responsible government, but to insist that ultimate authority lay with the Crown, which in practice was himself, as governor in Canada. The government resigned, as is proper in a parliamentary system under this circumstance. Notably, MacNab remained moderate. He was happy there was a strong governor in place, but reluctant to

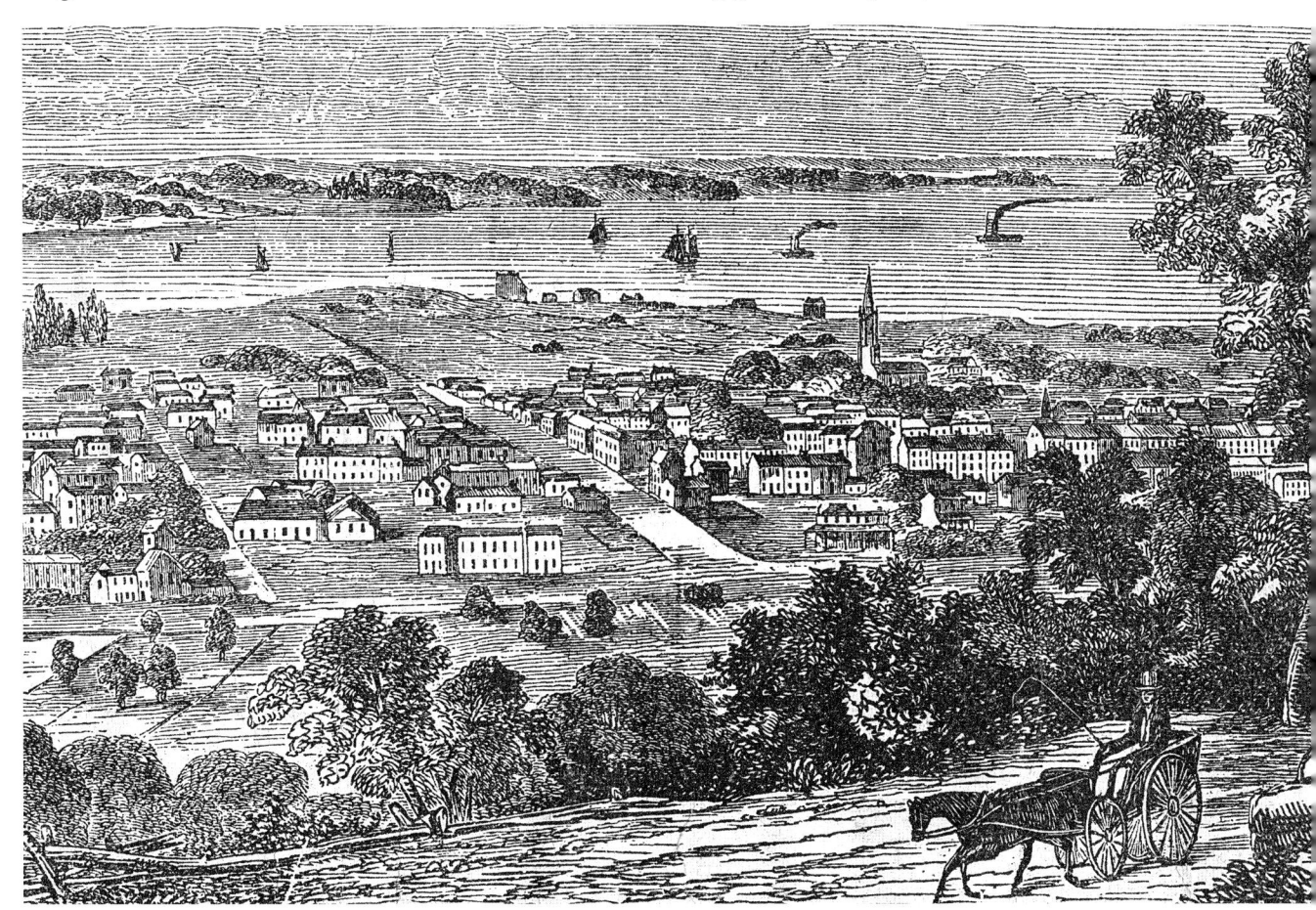

View of Hamilton, 1845, looking east from the Bay Street bridge over the railway

upset the new political system. Metcalfe constructed a new Council, without MacNab, although with MacNab's support.

In the election of the fall of 1844, Sir Allan's local popularity held firm and he was easily re-elected to Hamilton. Further success followed with his election as Speaker of the Assembly in late 1844, despite his inability to speak French, now an issue in Canadian politics. His support for Metcalfe, his friendships with Lower Canadians, and his long experience as Speaker in the old Upper Canada won the day. MacNab proved to be a superb Speaker, upholding and reinforcing parliamentary tradition and privileges, adding books to the parliamentary library, and most importantly, showing evident impartiality in his rulings, and doing all this with great dignity. This complex man was passionate about impartiality in this role. While the legislature was in session in Montreal, MacNab brought his family with him. Here Lady Mary introduced Anne Jane, her step-daughter, to society. Their own younger daughters, Sophia and Minnie, came too, that they might benefit from exposure to the older, more settled and genteel society, and instruction available to young girls in Montreal.

Lady MacNab's health began now to deteriorate significantly. Sir Allan took her to England in 1845, hoping the voyage, perhaps the sea air, would improve her health. Sophia accompanied them, but more for her mother than her father, as Sir Allan had railway business on his mind. He was also considering leaving politics, and was angling for a new position as adjutant general for the Canadas, charged with reorganizing the militia. He was seeking a baronetcy as well, the next level up in the aristocratic pecking order. A knighthood was a considerable honour, a reward for faithful service, but a baronetcy was hereditary, and would have conferred honour on his daughters and future generations of the MacNab branch.

The colonial office authorities refused even to meet MacNab. Added to this disappointment, Mary's condition — a disease untreatable, really, until the late twentieth century — became worse. Sir Allan returned to Dundurn with a successful sale of stock in the Great Western Railway project and a mace for the legislature in hand, but without any of his other purposes accomplished. In March, he went to attend the session of the legislature, determined to be present when the new governor, Lord Cathcart, arrived to replace the ailing Metcalfe. He was soon called home urgently by his daughter Anne Jane and his sister-in-law Sophia. Lady Mary's condition was now grave. There was a little time for family lightness still left, however. Sophia, thirteen, mentioned in her diary that her father purchased two dogs for her and Minnie, and Lady Mary named them Fin and Finette — Fin, from the French for fine, small or delicate, and Finette probably a play on the word for the female of the pair. All the family were delighted to have some joy introduced into a house waiting on death. While the girls played in the spring sunshine with their new pets, Sir Allan kept busy redesigning the gardens and grounds with William Reid, his gardener. Partly this was also to distract his daughters, as Reid organized garden plots for the two girls.

Sir Allan and Lady Mary were able to enjoy a last taste of companionship, spending hours discussing the improvements to the grounds. A few weeks later, on May 8, she died, her family around her. The sorrow of the family was poignantly expressed by Sophia in her diary, who ended the account of her mother's final moments saying simply "I can write no more." Lady MacNab's funeral was fit for the wife of the head of the MacNabs of Dundurn. A long procession of mourners, many of them local people, especially women, both "Black and White" as little Sophia noted in her diary, walked from the house to the family plot on the grounds, Inchbuie, where Mary was laid to rest.

Eight days later, MacNab had to return to Montreal to sit in the Speaker's chair, as several important bills were coming before the legislature. He decided to assuage his grief and that of his family by bringing them to Montreal, and then, when the session ended, to Quebec. In both places there was much to do, even given the social rules surrounding mourning in those days, as well as many extended family members and friends to visit. The trip, which lasted into the summer, was a success according to Sophia, who had begun to write in her diary again. They viewed a military parade, visited country houses, and attended a memorial of the Battle of Waterloo on the Plains of Abraham.

The two younger girls were allowed to stay up later than at home — even 9 p.m. on one occasion, Sophia noted — and frequently arrived back after Sir Allan had returned from his workday in the legislature. They spent much time visiting a convent — an orphanage for girls run by nuns — where they brought little gifts of candy to the girls and attended a confirmation ceremony. They attended church frequently, this being Catholic Montreal as opposed to little Hamilton with its one parish church, often inconvenient to attend given the bad roads. While there, the girls and their Aunt Sophia left Sir Allan to take a side trip to Quebec City.

On their return to Hamilton, MacNab decided he had to redecorate and renovate Dundurn. Little had been done to it since its completion in 1835, and work was necessary. Robert Wetherell had died in 1845, so MacNab sought out another architect. Henry Bower Lane, who had a long practice in England behind him, and hired him. He was a good choice as he designed improvements that were in keeping with the original vision Wetherell and MacNab had shared in the 1830s. More importantly, the work was a diversion for MacNab.

Sir John A. Macdonald, circa 1842–1843

MacNab's political fortunes seemed to decline further as the 1840s progressed. He was bypassed more and more in the legislature by newcomers such as John A. Macdonald. MacNab had been Speaker of the House since 1845, but lost that post in 1848 as the moderate Conservatives attempted to hold onto power by appointing a bilingual person as Speaker. The year 1848 was also a year of economic depression as the end of protected status for Canadian grain hit the econ-

Burning of Parliament, Montreal, 1849 painted by C.W. Jefferys (1869–1951) in 1911

omy. MacNab again found himself sitting in the legislature, this time as nominal leader of the opposition Conservatives.

Bills piled up on Sir Allan's desk as he continued the renovation work on Dundurn. He found a means to mortgage Dundurn in order to pay the bills, borrowing against the security of money left to his daughters. The next year, 1849, began with a new governor, Lord Elgin, who for the first time read the throne speech in both English and French.

MacNab was angered by the passage of the Rebellion Losses Bill, that same year, which compensated property owners, even the rebels themselves, for losses in the Rebellion of 1837. Tories in Montreal began to talk of seeking annexation by the United States, as they felt abandoned by Britain. They hoped to persuade Elgin not to sign the bill into law, using the royal prerogative, but the governor stuck closely to the principles of responsible government and made his way through a hostile Tory mob to the legislature. He returned through the same after signing the bill, and the mob turned its fury on the legislature, setting it on fire. MacNab did not approve of arson or uncontrolled mobs, and led several supporters into the burning building to rescue what they could — books from the library he had helped build, a portrait of the Queen, and the mace he had purchased in London.

He travelled to London to make the case for disallowing the Rebellion Losses Bill — which he failed at, but he did do some business for his rail projects. On his return he came out publicly against any talk of annexation. In the fall of that very busy year 1849, there was a family celebration when his eldest daughter, Anne Jane, married J.S. Davenport in Montreal. The Davenports were an old, aristocratic English family, further cementing MacNab's social position. But 1850 was a different matter, being a year of relative inactivity for MacNab, who was ill with gout and rheumatoid arthritis, which he nursed in the comfort of Dundurn. His mounting debts could not have helped his condition, nor his ongoing lack of political influence. He turned increasingly to his railroad projects. This technology of the day appealed to his sense of adventure and to his sense of its possibilities to earn great sums of money to maintain his lifestyle as a lord in his great house. If he was unimportant politically, he could at least pursue this.

"All My Politics Are Railroads"

Sir Allan Napier MacNab said over two bottles of port in 1851, "All my politics are railroads." Port bottles in the nineteenth century were much smaller than they are today, and the better known, if debatable, adage is *in vino veritas*, but in this case the drink did speak truly, whatever the size of the bottles.

MacNab's political defeats had at least allowed him time to concentrate on his newly revived interest in railroads. He had used his social and political visits to Britain since the 1840s to raise capital and technical support for his railroad ventures. Technologically, Britain was the most advanced nation in this area, and also the richest nation on earth, with investors ready and willing to promote railroad development throughout the British Empire and beyond. The last stages of his wife's illness in 1846, which forced him home from the legislature then sitting in Montreal to her bedside, also forced him to find life in work nearer home. He became involved in a succession of railway ventures, the most notable being the Great Western Railway (GWR), which was to form Canada's first complete rail system. Others were a branch of the GWR, called the Hamilton & Toronto, the Galt & Guelph, the Hamilton & Port Dover, and a kind of transportation conglomerate called the

Great Western Railway shops

Great Western Railway locomotive

North-West Transportation, Navigation and Railway Company.

In the 1840s, he turned his considerable energies to promoting the Great Western — blocking proposed rival railway companies and raising capital at home and in Britain. British capital was often in the form of bonds, rather than stocks, which left control of the companies in local hands — at least so long as they were profitable. His only fruitful political activity was linked to his railroad promotion — he served as chair of the railroad committee of the legislature from 1848 to 1857. Today, it is perhaps difficult to imagine the importance of railroads to Canada, to Hamilton, and to the western world in general. This was the leading edge transportation technology of the day — as important as air travel, superhighways, and the space program combined are to us. Governments and communities fought over having the railroad pass through or nearby and investors poured money into projects in a fashion not seen until the computer revolution. If Allan MacNab were alive in the twenty-first century, one could easily imagine him investing in airlines and software firms at a great and eager rate. Then, it was railroads.

The 1834 Act of the legislature which had incorporated and chartered the London and Gore Railway Company was revived and amended in 1845, to charter the Great Western Railway Company, with the authority to build a line from the Detroit River to Niagara, passing through

"All My Politics Are Railroads"

London, Brantford, and Hamilton. The next year, Hamilton, soon to be the centre of a rail system, incorporated as a city. Hamilton was still a commercial centre, but the arrival of the railroad shops began its transition to an industrial centre — a transformation that most likely would never have happened had not a young lawyer decided to set up shop in a small village at the head of Lake Ontario twenty years before. A rail link between the American border at Niagara and Michigan was made urgent by larger developments. There were supporters in the United States who saw a Canadian route as more sensible than one to the south of Lake Erie. MacNab worked tirelessly on his trips to Britain to raise capital. His skills at squeezing financial blood from stones, honed since his arrival in Hamilton as a young barrister, were invaluable in this period, but were to prove his undoing soon.

Ground for the new railroad was broken cere-

Great Western Railway station, by W.T. Smedley

Opening of the Great Western Railway station in London; 1854 woodcut as seen in The Illustrated London News, *January 21, 1854*

monially in London, Ontario, in 1847. MacNab was ill again, but the occasion suited his sense of theatre. Saturday, October 23, was a clear, beautiful fall day. The town was unusually crowded and shops closed at noon for the show. Sir Allan and the local patriarch, Colonel Thomas Talbot, headed a procession that included the Rifle Company and the Royal Artillery, a band, local dignitaries, the Temperance society, and the Freemasons. A crowd of three thousand — nearly half the population of London — watched and cheered. Everyone knew, by 1847, that a railroad meant prosperity for any community anywhere in the world. In a space cleared from surrounding forest, and equipped with bleachers for spectators, Thomas Talbot turned the first sod.

Some were skeptical about the railroad's prospects, as another depression followed almost immediately when the demand for Canadian wheat collapsed for a time. This was a harsh reminder that the Canadian economy was still commercial and agricultural, whatever local citizens might dream, and commerce had to support this turn to railways and technology. This same year saw large numbers of Irish entering Canada to escape the famine, their arrival further taxing resources, and deepening the economic recession.

The 1845 Act chartering the Great Western had authorized £1.5 million capital stock at £25 per share for 60,000 shares. Locally, 5,000 shares were taken up; the rest was raised in Britain, principally by MacNab. The Act was generous in other ways: four years were allowed to raise capital for construction, and the company had the right to expropriate land when needed. It was required to carry mail, police, and armed forces, at a rate to be determined by the government. MacNab was voted president. In 1846, the power of the British backers was increased, when an oversight committee of eleven was appointed and given extensive powers. The result was that Canadian directors like MacNab had control over the day-to-day work of the railroad and seeing to political backing in Canada, while overall financial control resided in England. MacNab pulled all the strings he could to alter this, but financial realities blocked him. This was necessary, given that 90 percent of the funding and almost all the technical expertise came from Britain. The power to appoint the president also sat with the committee of eleven — perhaps explaining MacNab's trips to Britain in this period as he attempted to influence the British owners in his favour.

Ground may have been broken in 1847, but by 1848 the recession had stopped all work as money dried up. In 1849, an Act of the legislature to guarantee bonds of railway companies helped the situation. Despite its being proposed by the Reform government, and despite its evident shortcomings, MacNab, the leader of the Tory opposition, supported this Bill enthusiastically. The Act only provided government financial guarantees — not actual cash — for rail companies with at least 75 miles of track laid, and which were half completed, and even then the guarantees were for only half the total cost of construction. But the Great Western was the only line in British North America close to fulfilling these requirements, and an important principle was established — that government should stand behind private enterprise in this country. Nothing was to stand in the way of development, especially development that benefited Sir Allan's position in society.

MacNab's railroad (as it must be called, for it would never have existed without his talents), the Great Western, was now operational too, although not fully completed. Its yards and shops were clearly visible from the front acreage of Dundurn. Dundurn no longer looked out onto an untrammelled view of woods and bay — though these were still here — but the belching shops of the railroad intervened below where Richard Beasley's wharf and log home had once existed. MacNab had created that peculiar ambience which marks Hamilton to this day — of wild woods and heavy industry existing almost side by side.

MacNab, however, was himself forced out of the presidency of the Great Western by 1849, due to some sharp practices — or, more precisely, because he was caught, since his dealings were not at all unusual. Stock could be sold to investors for just a small down payment — contingent on the company asking the investor to put up more, or even the balance of the stock held on paper when funds were needed for development. MacNab made huge profits selling shares to investors in this fashion but another of the roller-coaster economic slumps, this one beginning in 1848, meant that calls for further payments on the stock were ignored by the shareholders, leaving the company short.

After the passage of the Rebellion Losses Bill in 1849, MacNab began to draw back from the extremes of his party, while still not favouring the opposite extremes of the reformers who were calling for full independence from Britain. His newly moderate stance began to bring him back into the good graces of the imperial authorities. While his former allies among the Tories continued to rage against the move to responsible government and the Rebellion Losses Bill, MacNab began to feel more comfortable with moderate reformers, even with his old opponent Baldwin, who had come into power with the advent of responsible government, and was now a leading figure in the Canadas. Sir Allan had become convinced that the new form of government was here to stay and that practicality dictated he must live and work within the new system. And so he did; in March 1851 he very publicly shook hands with Governor General Lord Elgin in front of a crowd assembled for a festival celebrating the Hamilton Mechanics' Institute. The crowd applauded. Was this a new MacNab? Perhaps, but perhaps not. MacNab was pragmatic in everything except maintaining his place in the social order. In the 1830s the old Family Compact was the way to advance; now in the 1850s supporting a British–style democratic constitution was the reality. It would not help his place in the British Canadian world if MacNab constantly flouted and fought the established order, and certainly it would not help his railroad promotion schemes.

At the same time, MacNab, now in his early fifties, was feeling his age and worrying about leaving his family in financial difficulty. He sharpened, as it were, his already shady business practices, despite the setback with the Great Western. He began to make very large profits indeed by selling lands to the Great Western as construction moved through land he owned, even where better routes were available. In 1850, although he was very ill with gout most of the year, his influence was still great enough to ensure the passage of an act that allowed municipalities to subscribe stock in railway companies. Hamilton invested £50,000 in the Great

Above: The first locomotive with a steel boiler, lithograph by J. Ottman Lithographic Co., Montreal, 1861
Opposite page: Great Western Railway yards below Dundurn, 1850s

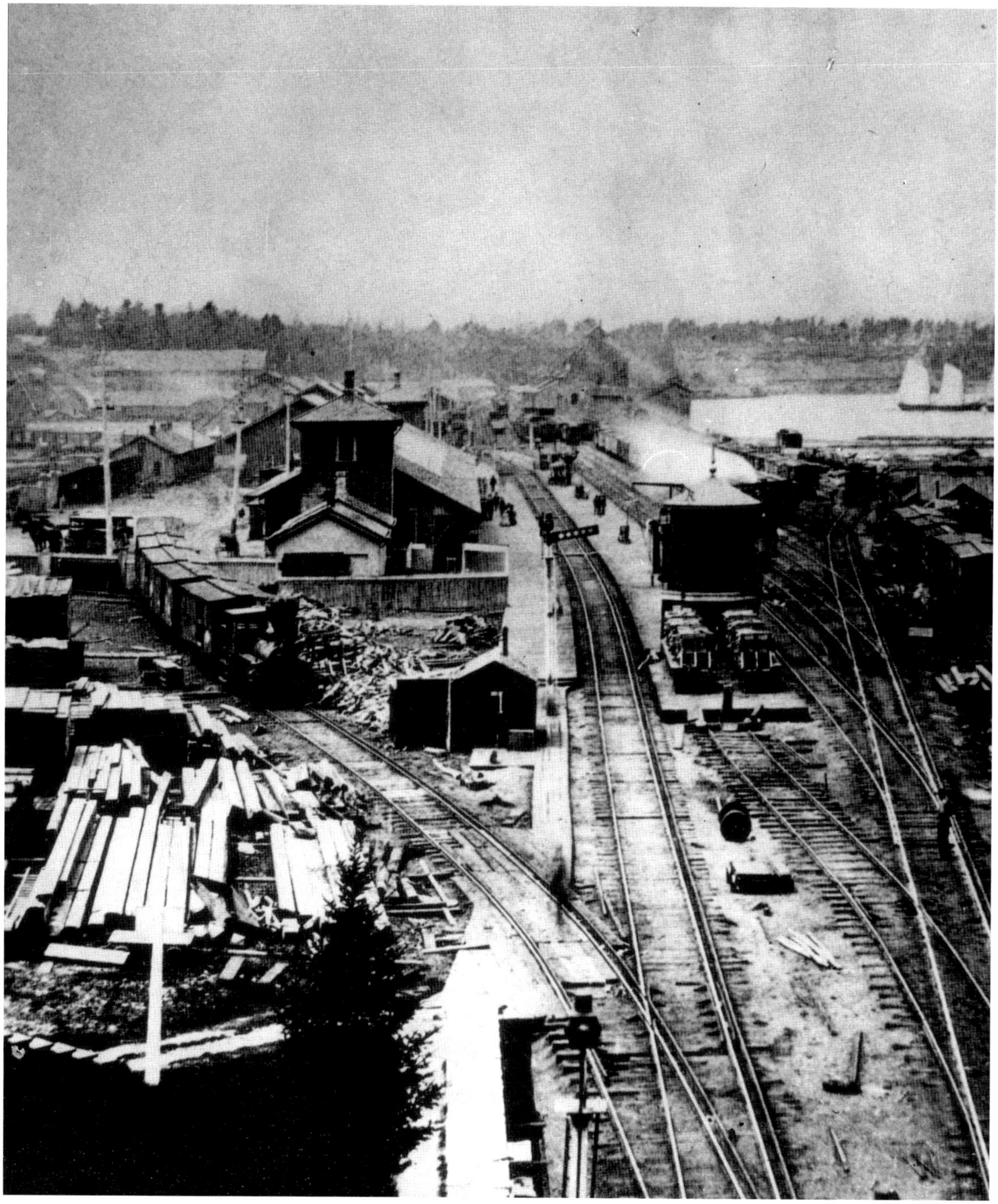

Western. Costs had spiralled — the initial estimate of £1.5 million, or about $6 million, reached $25 million by the railroad's completion in 1858. Some of the costs were a result of the number of construction projects in competition, while others were a result of the difficulties of driving a line over the Desjardins Canal and up the Niagara Escarpment. Some were, however, a result of inflated land purchases from MacNab himself, as well as others. In one instance, MacNab, in a characteristically murky affair, apparently attempted to deceive his fellow directors in order to improve his own financial gain.

The Great Western, although usually undercapitalized, managed in the early 1850s to arrange enough investment capital in Canada, the United States, and Britain to complete the line and start traffic. They attempted to rid themselves utterly of MacNab in 1854 by promising him a £5,000 bonus to resign his directorship. There was irony here, as this year marked the full opening of the line from Niagara to Windsor. MacNab accepted the offer from Great Western, to what must have been their great relief. They could, now more than ever, ill afford to flout someone who had much say in patronage, the grease of politics then and now. MacNab, as a result of his gradual move to moderation, had become premier of the Canadas — the summit of Canadian politics.

Premier Sir Allan Napier MacNab then joined Great Western's better-financed rival, the Grand Trunk Railway, which was promoted by Montreal and Toronto interests. MacNab, in what was unusual speed, received the £5,000 from Great Western in 1855. All through this period he was increasingly afflicted with pain from gout, which dulled his formerly acute political and financial instincts. By now, his short premiership was nearly at an end, as younger and equally moderate Tories headed by John A. Macdonald had managed to reorganize within the divided legislature and were now determined to force the old knight out. John A. Macdonald formed a new government, with all of the old members except MacNab. Later in 1856 he was forced out of his directorship in the Grand Trunk, his influence and thus usefulness to that company at an end, as it was for the government also.

The next year, the Great Western offered him another £6,000 for help in countering a rival line called the Canada Southern, being constructed to compete directly with the GWR's route to Michigan. Apparently they still respected Sir Allan's political and promotional abilities to a degree, but there were also some strange negotiations behind the scenes. The Great Western had by this time two boards of directors — one in Canada and one in England. The English board controlled the Canadian one normally, but seems to have looked the other way in this instance. Their worry was that the Canada Southern line would be built to the south of the Great Western, undercutting its business, which was principally in carrying American freight between New York State and Michigan. Isaac Buchanan, another Hamilton entrepreneur, who had no formal connection with the Great Western, became involved in some murky fashion. MacNab was paid by Buchanan to isolate and negate this threat. The end result of this still dark and complex affair was the dismissal and replacement of the Canadian board and the imposition of even greater control by the British owners. But MacNab wisely took the money, quickly. There was some rumbling that he might be sued to regain the payment, but the matter was dropped for unknown reasons. It was then Sir Allan received word he had been given a baronetcy (a hereditary knighthood). He sailed to England for a visit, then returned and resigned his seat in the legislature. Apparently he meant to settle in England, and began to wind up his affairs.

MacNab was not deterred from promoting railroads, however. In 1856 he revived the idea of

View of the Desjardins Canal railway bridge, Hamilton, the morning of the Great Western Railway disaster of March 12, 1857, when 59 lives were lost, engraving by H. Gregory and D.N. Preston

a line from Hamilton to Port Dover on Lake Erie. Capital was subscribed by the city of Hamilton, the town of Caledonia, and private individuals, and a survey and construction were begun. This unusual proceeding was made possible by the bill in the legislature that allowed municipalities to invest directly in railroads — a gamble in good times that would prove disastrous in bad.

A major depression hit Canada, turning 1857 into another dark year financially — and his sojourn in the Old Country had cost a lot. He found himself reduced to asking friends for enough money to keep up appearances. He was unable to gain anything for the new railroad scheme started before his departure from Canada, as this recession was affecting the British economy also. He managed to return to Canada. The Hamilton he returned to had gone bankrupt, leading to a comic opera scene in which the municipal tax rolls disappeared with a city official, so the sheriff could not levy a special tax to pay the city's debt. This was by far the worst economic downturn Canada had experienced ever, affecting much of the province.

The depression of 1857 had halted work on the new railroad — indeed, the £50,000 Hamilton had given was partially responsible for the city's own bankruptcy that year. The economy once again recovered, but the market for rail lines was now saturated and needed to wait on further growth in population and in the economy before being reborn. The project was finally to be completed, but not until the 1870s, after MacNab's death. Yet Sir Allan seemed refreshed and in better health, and set to work to revive his situation. Sir Allan MacNab, Baronet, through his rail promotions, had altered the landscape of southern Ontario, creating the seeds of an industrial city in Hamilton, and providing a lucrative carrying trade that brought prosperity to other cities along the route. Much of the urban landscape of southwestern Ontario can be traced by following the line of the Great Western Railway — from Niagara, to Hamilton, west to London and on to Windsor.

View of Hamilton, 1860

MacNab the Moderate

Sir Allan's whole life was not bound up in railroad development and politics. He was happily involved in other events also. There had been changes in the lives of the other residents of Dundurn. In 1842, his sister Anna Maria had married Alexander Stewart, and had left the castle to set up her married home nearby with her new husband and his two children from his first marriage. Hannah Mary, another of MacNab's sisters, went to live with the newlyweds. The youngest sister, Lucy, had married his law partner J. O. Hatt in 1837. Then there was the marriage of his eldest daughter, the last of his first family with Elizabeth Brooke. Anne Jane's marriage to John Salisbury Davenport, a British army officer, at Christ Church in Montreal in 1849, considerably lightened the laird's life in this difficult period, although it did also mean that he was only to see his eldest daughter occasionally, as her husband was frequently posted to the far parts of the Empire.

Sir Allan was also active in his church, attending the first synod of the Church of England in Canada West, in Toronto in 1853, where he voted to retain the Clergy Reserves for the church, though this was more a matter of form, than of any deep conviction, as he had always believed these lands should be apportioned to the benefit of all churches. In the early 1850s he attended the laying of a cornerstone for Trinity College, built to replace the institution lost to the secular University of Toronto, and observed more than participated in the life of the legislature, which now met in Quebec.

The year 1852 saw the beginning of a new monument at Queenston Heights to Sir Isaac Brock, the victor of the battle there over the Americans in the War of 1812. The original statue had been destroyed by one of the rebels of 1837 in a bomb planted in 1840. MacNab became involved in the campaign to raise funds to rebuild. Economic problems meant the project stayed on the back burner until 1852, when at last reconstruction began. Unusually, he was

Sir Allan MacNab, circa 1850

House of Assembly, North Front, Quebec, watercolour by Mary Millicent Chaplin (1790–1858)

harshly criticized locally for his involvement — many believed there was corruption involved, but a simpler and truer explanation was the constant roller-coaster nature of the economy that made collecting money for less than pragmatic projects very difficult. Times must have indeed been tight, as this was exactly the kind of display MacNab loved deeply.

By 1854, Allan MacNab was seen as a moderate Tory, capable of holding in check the more extreme conservative element, which used to count him as a member, and also the extreme liberal element. On the way to the first session of 1854, he found himself on the same ship as William Lyon Mackenzie, his old rival. The two were older now, and cordial, former warriors in a world where they were fast being made redundant. They had even found themselves on the same side of a vote favouring representation by population — Canada West was now beginning to pass Canada East in numbers and wanted to upset the balance of power legislated between the two halves.

MacNab had discovered a truth that has governed Canada as a whole ever since — successful governments hold power through the middle. The trick, of course, is in finding the middle at any particular time, as it tends to shift. Mackenzie thought MacNab might again be elected Speaker, and praised his past record in this post in a speech to the legislature. The 1830s were indeed dead and gone. The legislature was so divided that neither side could form a government. The result: MacNab became premier of the Canadas, heading a moderate coalition from 1854 to 1856. This was, as far as his party was concerned, a temporary expedient, lasting only until a way out of political impasse could be found.

For the time being, Premier MacNab, the old gouty laird, would hold things together. Two important issues were dealt with in this period — issues that earlier had aroused great passions, but now most were tired and wanted them finished. First was the final settlement of the Clergy Reserves in the old Upper Canada, now Canada West. These lands had been set aside for the "support of a Protestant clergy" when Upper Canada was first surveyed. Disputes arose over which Protestant church should benefit, and over the fact that most of the lands remained wild, even in areas with heavy population pressure. By 1854, it had been agreed that the Church of England and the Church of Scotland were the proper beneficiaries, receiving half the revenue from sales, while the other Protestants divided the other half.

The Anglicans, headed by Bishop Strachan of Toronto, wanted them finally disposed of now that responsible government was a fact. The bishop feared that non-Anglicans would have a say in the affairs of his church if it were not fully cut off from state funding through the Reserves. The Church of Scotland had split in the 1840s into different competing groups, making the division of proceeds even more complex. The Clergy Reserves Bill of 1856 settled this issue finally by fully secularizing the Reserves, putting proceeds from sales to a municipal development fund, and some revenues into commutation funds that would pay money to clergy already in receipt of funds from this source. The other issue was particular to Lower Canada — the winding up of the last feudal remnant of New France, seigneurial tenure. Both measures passed easily.

A young man entered MacNab's personal life in this period. William Coutts Keppel, Viscount Bury, although only twenty-two years old, was appointed Superintendent of Indian Affairs by the Imperial government. MacNab was doubtful that one so young could be competent in this post, but Bury's easy and friendly character won the laird over quickly. He moved next door to MacNab's residence in the capital Toronto, and there met Sophia MacNab. They were to marry, eventually, and Sophia Mary MacNab was to find herself the wife of the 7th Earl of Albemarle when the young man succeeded to his father's title. When Bury began courting Sophia, Sir Allan decided it was time to spruce up Dundurn. He hired the architect Frederick Rastrick to design a portico for the York Street entrance. This was to be an entrance fit not only for a prime minister, but also to receive guests and potential family members as important as Viscount Bury. The courting was successful, and the wedding had to be at Dundurn. This necessitated more work, inside this time. There would be two ceremonies, as Sophia was Catholic like her mother, but Bury of course Church of England. It was now that MacNab began to call Dundurn "Dundurn Castle."

The first, Catholic, wedding ceremony took place early in the morning of November 15, 1855, and the second, Church of England, service, was celebrated by the bishop of Toronto, John Strachan, at eleven o'clock in the drawing room of the castle. Later that evening there was a ball in the same room. Dundurn, after the newlyweds and all the guests had left, was smaller somehow, with only Allan, his sister-in-law, Sophia, and his youngest daughter, Minnie, living there now. Aunt Sophia and Allan agreed that Minnie should now enter society to find a suitable husband. Sophia insisted that this man should be Catholic.

On May 18, 1856, MacNab's premiership was all but over. John A. Macdonald sent a letter to Dundurn on that date informing MacNab bluntly that he should resign or the government would resign, forcing him out. His party no longer needed him and had decided to discard him as quickly as possible. Premier MacNab resigned along with the other members of the government, knowing that they would then regroup and form a new government without him. MacNab was so ill he had to be carried into the legislature in the spring of 1856 to make his final speech as premier after the rest of the government had resigned. All the same members except MacNab entered the "new" government. He returned to the legislature, this time as a private member, free now to vote his conscience.

After spending the early summer at Dundurn, MacNab sailed for England, where he purchased a house with a mortgage (as usual). Apparently he was considering leaving Canada entirely to retire to the centre of empire, a habit other, later, Canadian politicians were to imitate. He returned briefly to Canada where he laid the cornerstone of Victoria Hall in Cobourg, in his capacity as Masonic Grand Master. His involvement in the Masons was another of those activities where MacNab was pragmatic, rather than dogmatic. Men of business in those days belonged usually to an array of clubs and organizations. This was where much of the wheeling and dealing was done, behind the closed doors and oaths of secrecy.

Viscount Bury had lost his position as Superintendent of Indian Affairs, because the office was now turned over to Canada. He and Sophia decided to move to England, where Bury would stand for parliament. They wanted Sir Allan to go with them. His daughter Anne Jane was there now too, and he had only to move himself, Aunt Sophia, and Minnie. But he did not want to abandon Dundurn. However, at the end of that year, he resigned his seat, announcing he was heading to England. Although too ill to attend a dinner held in his honour, he received an address of appreciation from city council. He did attend a farewell dinner at the Mechanics' Institute in early December. He spoke emotionally about past and present to a large crowd. Then, in a kind of royal "progress," the mayor and council and a crowd accompanied him to the railway station to see him off.

In England, he found that his son-in-law Viscount Bury had won election to parliament and he spent a happy Christmas of 1857 with his daughter and family. Honours followed in the new year. On February 5, he was invested baronet, and presented to Queen Victoria on February 18. He was made an honorary aide-de-camp to the Queen, and an honorary colonel in the British Army. While in Britain, he spent time in London and in the resort town of Brighton. He had arrived, finally, meeting and moving with the highest ranks of the British Conservative Party — both because of the contacts he had made over his years of promoting Canadian railroads and because his son-in-law, Lord Bury, the husband of little Sophia the diarist, introduced him to the society he had always aspired to join.

Refreshed, he returned to Canada and Dundurn in July. His finances had been in more disorder than usual because of a sharp recession that struck Canada in the late 1850s, but it had been brief, and already business was improving. He seemed to have recovered his old vigour too, and soon was able to set his financial affairs on an even keel again. He and his son-in-law had conceived the idea that the Atlantic crossing could be improved by having faster, new steamships sailing from Ireland. The company was called the Atlantic Steam Navigation Company. MacNab returned again to the British Isles, to survey prospects in Ireland. Suffering again from gout, he went to the seaside resort of Brighton to recuperate. He liked the place so much, that, on a whim, he decided to stand for election to the Westminster parliament there. He had no chance, of course, as both the sitting members had held the seats for a long time and

Dundurn Castle postcard, circa 1900

were popular, but a victory would no doubt have meant his permanent removal from Canada.

He returned again to Hamilton, thinking this a temporary visit to put his affairs in better order. Business had deteriorated again, and his income in classic fashion did not meet his expenses. He owed money on mortgages, and was owed, but the two did not balance. Standing for election in Britain must also have been expensive. His business dealings were so complex that he was able to forestall creditors daunted by this sheer complexity.

In 1860 he found his honorary position as aide-de-camp to the Queen had some actual duty attached to it. That year, the Prince of Wales was sent on a tour of Canada, and MacNab accompanied him as an aide-de-camp. He met the prince at Quebec, then travelled to the new and permanent capital at Bytown — now Ottawa — where the prince was to lay the cornerstone of the new parliament buildings. The prince moved through Canada West, arriving in Hamilton, where he stayed at Dundurn. The castle and MacNab had clearly arrived at a point of which even Sir Allan could not have dreamed in the 1820s.

The visit over, MacNab was again (or still) in financial difficulties, being sued this time by the Bank of Upper Canada. He was warned by his friend the local sheriff that his furniture might be seized. Included in this letter to MacNab from the sheriff was a request for help from MacNab in gaining a promotion in the local regiment. MacNab called on the sheriff, who came out of the pleasant visit having advanced a loan to MacNab to forestall having his furniture seized. This gave MacNab time to vest his furniture in his daughter Minnie's name, and to raise another mortgage to pay the sheriff back.

MacNab returned now to politics. He ran for the legislative council this time, in the Windsor area, and won, despite being so ill with gout that he hardly campaigned at all. He continued his political and business activities, holding together his incredible conglomeration of land holdings, directorships, mortgages, and loans in a balancing act he had perfected over more than thirty years. He heard that the government was going to build an asylum for deaf mutes, and lobbied hard to have it located in Hamilton. He had a good piece of land that he considered perfect as a site for the asylum. He needed money for another wedding, too. His daughter Minnie had finally met her lifemate while living with her father in Quebec, where the Assembly was still sitting until Ottawa was ready. This was John George Daly, the son of MacNab's old friend and colleague Dominick. Dominick had just been appointed governor of South Australia, and his son was to accompany him as secretary. They were married at St. Mary's Catholic Cathedral in Hamilton by Bishop Farrell, and Sir Allan said goodbye to another part of his life.

The government stepped in at just the right moment to save MacNab. Two friends valued six acres of land offered for sale for the deaf mute asylum at the very high sum of $20,000. MacNab collected the money from the Bank of Upper Canada immediately, but it was a year before the government actually authorized its payment.

The story is that, on his deathbed, the old baronet raised himself up on one elbow and whispered with a force now nearly gone, "No more disputes." In 1862, death came to MacNab in his beloved Dundurn, after a life filled with disputes. Allan Napier MacNab was never a man to avoid controversy. He had lived life to the full, always a partisan without apology, driven by a sense of self and a need to be active on many levels. Today we venerate moderation. Not so Allan MacNab, who, like most of his generation, thought moderation a weakness. He was active until a few days before his death, travelling to Toronto on business, serving as a pall bearer for his old friend William Hamilton Merritt, signing election papers, and engaging in his most frequent activity, avoiding creditors.

Despite his final request, dispute surrounded his passing. Sir Allan was a member of the Church of England in Canada, a regular supporter of Christ's Church in Hamilton. Yet he was married for many years to a devout Roman Catholic, and his two daughters by her, Minnie and Sophia, were raised in that church. His sister-in-law Sophia Stuart claimed he had converted to Catholicism as he lay dying in his room at Dundurn. This was hotly disputed by John Gamble Geddes, his old friend and Anglican minister at Christ's Church, who claimed the "Romish" Bishop Farrell had stolen Sir Allan away from his rightful faith, claiming that MacNab had been unconscious at the end. The dispute has never been entirely untangled, though MacNab's biographer Donald Beer gives the balance of evidence to the Catholic side.

At first MacNab was buried in the family cemetery, Inchbuie, on the grounds of Dundurn. But many years later, after Dundurn passed into other hands, the controversy over the deathbed conversion still raging, his family was divided by religion — Sir Allan and his second wife being moved to Holy Sepulchre Catholic cemetery and his parents, first wife, and only son to the Protestant Hamilton cemetery. "Disputes" marked both death and life for Allan Napier MacNab.

Epilogue

Postcard of Dundurn Castle, circa 1900

Allan Napier MacNab, Bart., did leave a will, but along with it, a host of financial entanglements. His will, drawn up in 1860, called for annuities for his sister-in-law Sophia and for his sisters Anna Maria and Hannah. The remaining amount was to be invested and the interest divided among his daughters in a complex fashion. The problem was, he owed money to the Bank of Upper Canada, and to many other individuals. There were two trustees of the will, his sister-in-law Sophia and Thomas Street of Niagara, a business partner, the latter refusing to become involved, probably sensibly given the extreme complexity of Sir Allan's financial house of cards. Sophia did what she could, auctioning off all the contents of Dundurn in what must have been the auction sale of the century. His library of more than three hundred books was auctioned separately. MacNab had also set up marriage settlements for his daughters Sophia and Minnie. Henry John Boulton, his old friend, was trustee of this and brought suit against Aunt Sophia as trustee of the estate. Her only means to raise money was to sell Dundurn itself at auction. No one would, or could, buy it, so Aunt Sophia, with money from Lord Bury, bought the house, in effect from herself. MacNab would have approved of this sleight-of-hand. She then took out a mortgage and paid the monies owed. Sophia did not intend to live there, and moved to Australia, leaving it empty for four years.

Dundurn was then used as an institution for deaf mutes — that same organization Sir Allan had sold land for earlier. The house was dirty and in need of repair, which the superintendent decided was good therapy for the inmates to handle. Great fun was had in the legislature as a committee was convened in an attempt to discover why the land sold in 1860 was never used for the purpose, and why Dundurn had to be leased for the same reason later. Again, MacNab would have enjoyed this fight. After the asylum moved to Belleville, Sophia sold Dundurn, this time to a syndicate in the United States that planned some kind of spa resort. This did not come to be.

In 1872, the house again became a home, but for the last time. Donald McInnes, a member of the new industrial class in Hamilton, purchased the house and property and moved into it with his family. McInnes had the money to refurbish the house, and to make some alterations to suit the times and his family — the house lived again. In 1899, McInnes sold Dundurn to the city. He had threatened to demolish it and develop houses on the site. The city, in a mood reminiscent of MacNab, used a debenture to raise the purchase price of $150,000. Inchbuie had remained in MacNab family hands, now represented by a daughter of Minnie's. She sold it to the city also, and had the remains there moved, some to the Protestant Hamilton Cemetery and some to the Catholic Holy Sepulchre. Dundurn was later to become a city museum and even for a while to house a zoo in its grounds. In 1967, the house was restored to the year 1855.

The original restoration was planned as Hamilton's premiere centennial project, for Canada's 100th anniversary as a nation. Anthony Adamson, the well-known restoration architect, and Marion MacRae, an architectural historian, directed the restoration with the active assistance of local historians and the full support of the City of Hamilton. Restoration has not stopped, however, as Dundurn is still a living house. Recently, the dining room has been repainted to reflect new knowledge of colours used in 1855. A chair belonging to MacNab has been placed in the drawing room through the generosity of a local historian and archivist.

For us today, Allan Napier MacNab is something of a puzzle. He engaged in business practices which today are punished with jail time. Yet, he was noted for his generosity to the poor and even to defeated enemies. His character was formed before the reign of Queen Victoria and the sense of order and propriety we associate with her name. Yet Sir Allan had made an impact on his world which is felt even today. In politics, he is regarded as a minor figure, one suspects mostly because he was not part of the story of Confederation. But he did exemplify his times.

Beginning as a man seeking admission to the ruling Family Compact in the 1820s and 1830s, he moved gradually towards a moderate position politically as the new, democratic order established in 1840 became obviously irreversible. He was, as always, concerned to build the MacNab family fortune and name with his New-World Dundurn as its physical expression. He succeeded in this goal, but the means needed brought him into the technological civilization of the Victorian era. He remained the bluff, hearty eighteenth-century country squire in his character and attitudes. Sir Allan MacNab is too often overshadowed by luminaries such as Sir John A. MacDonald, but he laid the foundations for the industrial city of Hamilton, and, through his major creation the Great Western Railway, he can be credited with laying the foundations of prosperity for much of southern Ontario.

Acknowledgements

Most books are collaborative efforts and this is no exception. A number of printed sources were consulted, but the book could not have been written without the help and advice of Hamilton historians. Margaret Houghton, archivist and head of Special Collections at the Hamilton Public Library, generously shared her seemingly inexhaustible knowledge of sources. Her guidance cut short long hours searching for historical pictures of the castle and Hamilton. At Dundurn National Historic Site, Ian Kerr-Wilson, the curator, allowed me to wander the castle and ask many questions about details, no matter how small. Especially helpful was Tom Minnes, the curatorial assistant who shared his long knowledge of the house and of Sir Allan and his family.

Rob Skeoch's photographs perfectly capture Dundurn in a manner that takes one back to the nineteenth century. The exterior is stunning, and his interior pictures bring the old house to life again, from top to bottom.

The editorial staff at James Lorimer & Company have been helpful and patient. Lynn Schellenberg put up with my academic pace with good humour and expert prompting, and saved me from my own worst excesses of purple prose. Catherine MacIntosh expertly guided the project to completion.

Cockpit before restoration

Cockpit after restoration

Sources

There are a large number of works on the life of Sir Allan MacNab, and several on his great house, Dundurn Castle. The standard biography is Donald Beer's book, and the best book on the house itself is Marion MacRae's, which weaves together Sir Allan's life with the life of the Castle. The Hamilton Public Library's Special Collections department was consulted for its extensive clipping files, archival records, and books on Dundurn and Sir Allan MacNab. Below are the principal published works consulted.

Beer, Donald R. *Sir Allan Napier MacNab.* Hamilton, ON: Dictionary of Hamilton Biography, 1984.
Bourinot, John George. *Some Memories of Dundurn and Burlington Heights.* Royal Society of Canada, Transactions, Section II, 1900.
Carter, Charles Ambrose and Thomas Melville Bailey, eds. *The Diary of Sophia MacNab.* 2nd ed. revised. Hamilton, ON: W.L. Griffin Ltd., 1974.
Disher, J.W. and E.A.W. Smith. *By Design: The Role of the Engineer in the History of the Hamilton Burlington Area.* Hamilton, ON: Hamilton Engineering Interface Inc., 2001.
Innis, Mary Quayle, ed. *Mrs. Simcoe's Diary.* Toronto: Macmillan of Canada, 1965.
MacRae, Marion. *MacNab of Dundurn.* Toronto: Clarke, Irwin & Company Ltd., 1971.
Weaver, John C. *Hamilton: An Illustrated History.* Toronto: James Lorimer & Company, Publishers, 1982.

Photo Credits

Except for the following images, all photographs in this book were taken by Rob Skeoch at Dundurn National Historic Site and the Hamilton Military Museum, Hamilton, Ontario.

The publisher acknowledges with thanks the assistance of the collections and individuals who supplied the images appearing on the following pages:

Archives of Ontario: 54 (Government of Ontario Art Collection: AC694158); 83 (F 598, Archibald MacMillan fonds: 10003077)
Dundurn National Historic Site/City of Hamilton: 61
Hamilton Public Library, Special Collections: 6 above; 55; 56; 57; 60; 63; 64; 69; 70; 71; 75; 76; 77; 81; 84; 85; 90; 93 left; back cover bottom
James Lorimer & Company: 59 (photographed at Mackenzie House, Toronto, by Rob Skeoch)
Library and Archives Canada: 47 (Acc. No. R9266-75, Peter Winkworth Collection of Canadiana); 49 (C-013921); 50 (C-012703); 52 (C-024292); 53 above (C-095758); 66 (C-004788); 67 (C-121846); 73 (C-127864); 74 (C-073717); 78 (C-007770); 80 (Acc. No. R9266-3404, Peter Winkworth Collection of Canadiana); 86 (C-000823)
Thomas Minnes, private collection: 89, 91